Connect Across Disciplines Inquiry Projects

Introduction

The *Connect Across Disciplines Projects* are designed to deepen students' understanding of the Unit Concepts and Essential Questions through inquiry-based learning. The projects promote the integration of the strands of English language arts (reading, writing, speaking and listening, and language). They also promote the integration of language arts with content areas.

Inquiry-Based Learning
Each project presents an opportunity for students to investigate a real-world problem or challenge. While accomplishing each task, students develop 21st century skills, such as the use of technology, collaboration, communication, problem solving, critical thinking, innovation, and creativity.

The projects all share four main tasks:

Investigate
Students generate questions, make observations, explore, and research. They locate information through a variety of ways, including digital and paper sources and interviews. They engage in meaningful interactions with sources and with each other.

Create
Students create a product, which can include videos, audio recordings, journals, experiments, charts, graphs, maps, galleries, artworks, posters, flyers, and brochures, achieved both on paper and digitally.

Present
Students share their products with peers in many ways. They may present videos, role-plays, share a webpage, or guide a tour though an exhibition. The audiences are prompted to ask questions and the presenting groups provide answers and explanations.

Reflect and Respond
After projects are completed and presented, students reflect on what they have learned from their own experiences as well as what they have learned from presentations by other groups.

Assigning Projects and Roles
Students are more motivated when they engage in experiences that are relevant to their interests, everyday life, or important current events. You may wish to have students select which project they will work on based on their own personal interests. You may also wish to assign groups based on your social studies and science curriculum.

After students are organized into small groups, facilitate the efficacy of the project by assigning roles. Depending on the nature of the project, students may take on authentic roles such as Lead Researcher, Project Manager, Head Engineer, Main Presenter, Chief Designer, and so on.

©2018 Benchmark Education Company, LLC

UNIT 3
Essential Question: How do living things get what they need to survive?

SS Label a U.S. Map
ELA W.2.2, W.2.8, SL.2.1b, SL.2.2, SL.2.3, NGSS 2-LS4-1, 2-ESS2-2

Student Objectives
I will be able to:
- Conduct research to gather information about animals that are native to the United States.
- Label a map of the United States to show the names of the animals and their habitats.
- Create a legend for my map.

Materials
Internet sites such as the U.S. Fish and Wildlife Service • Copies of an outline map of the United States • Colored pencils

Investigate
- Guide students to gather information about animals that live in the United States and their natural habitats.
- Ask students to look for facts that identify and describe the places where these animals live.

Create
- Give each student a copy of an outline map of United States. Ask students to choose five of the animals they learned about and label each animal's habitat on the map. Encourage students to choose animals that live in a different places and habitats throughout the country.
- Students should include each animal's name and the name of the general area or location on the map. Ask students to draw a small picture of each animal as well.

Present
- Ask students to present their maps, name each animal and its habitat, and share one key detail about the animal or where it lives.
- Allow time for students to discuss the maps, specifically making comments about the information on the maps and linking their comments to others.

Reflect and Respond
- Ask students to reflect on what they learned about the diversity of animals and habitats within the United States.

NGSS Make a Habitat Mural
ELA W.2.2, W.2.7, W.2.8, W.2.10, SL.2.1c, SL.2.3, SL.2.6, NGSS 2-LS4-1

Student Objectives
I will be able to:
- Conduct research about the diverse habitats in the United States.
- Create a mural that features the physical landforms and plant and animal life in a specific habitat.

Materials
Internet sources such as the U. S. National Park Service • Butcher paper • Markers or colored pencils

Investigate
- Explain that the United States is home to a diversity of habitats. Use the U.S. National Park Service website to introduce students to a variety of national parks, such as Yellowstone, Zion, Redwood, Acadia, and Hot Springs.
- Instruct small groups to gather information about one of these national parks. Ask them to find facts that tell about the park's location, its unique physical features or landforms, and the plants and animals that live there.

Create
- Ask each group to create a mural that shows the key physical features of the habitat in the national park they learned about. Students should draw pictures of some of the plants and animals that live there and label them.
- Instruct students to title their mural and write a short description of the unique features of their national park.

Present
- Ask students to display their murals, and invite one member of each group to read the group's written description.
- Allow time for students in other groups to ask questions and clarify any information in the description or the mural. Remind students to ask and answer questions using complete sentences.

Reflect and Respond
- Ask students to reflect on the diversity represented in the mural and descriptions the class created. Encourage students to share new information and key details they learned about the United States and its many habitats. Guide students to make comparisons and contrasts between the various habitats depicted in the murals.

Connect Across Disciplines Inquiry Projects

 Create a Zoo Exhibit

ELA W.2.2, W.2.4, W.2.5, W.2.7, W.2.8, SL.2.1c, SL.2.3, SL.2.6, NGSS 2-LS4-1

Student Objectives
I will be able to:
- Use technology to gather information about a native animal from my state.
- Use written and visual information from various sources to create a model of the exhibit.

Materials
Internet sites such as the U.S. Fish and Wildlife Service and the USDA • Printer • Craft supplies (shoe boxes, socks, paper bags, yarn, felt, etc.) • Drawing materials

Investigate
- Ask small groups of students to research information about an animal that is native to the United States. Tell students to find information about the animal's physical characteristics, and habitat, and any other facts they find interesting or important.
- Ask students to find and print at least one picture of their animal as well as pictures that relate to any key information, such as what the animal eats or where it lives.

Create
- Students should discuss the facts they found and then use them to write a description of their animal. Ask students to include the kinds of information they would learn about their animal at a zoo.
- Ask students to use the pictures they printed and craft materials to create a model of their zoo exhibit. This could be a puppet, a drawing, a diorama, or another type of model. Remind students that zoos give information about their animals, and encourage students to include details that relate to the animal's appearance, habitat, and what it eats.
- Ask students to review their written description and determine if it clearly presents facts and details about their animal and its habitat.

Present
- Tell students to set up all of their zoo exhibits to form a miniature classroom zoo. Ask students to walk through the zoo and to learn about all the animals. Encourage them to ask questions to deepen their understanding of the animals.
- Ask a selected speaker from each group to read the written descriptions, point out key details in the diorama, and answer questions. Remind students to speak in complete sentences.

Reflect and Respond
- Ask students to choose one of the animals from the gallery and share an interesting fact they learned about it. Guide students to compare and contrast the various animals described in the exhibits.

Useful Resources
Even an Octopus Needs a Home by Irene Kelly
The Great Kapok Tree: A Tale of the Amazon Rain Forest by Lynne Cherry
A Strange Place to Call Home by Marilyn Singer and Ed Young
The Sea, the Storm, and the Mangrove Tangle by Lynne Cherry

CCSS for English Language Arts

ELA W.2.2 Write informative/explanatory texts in which they introduce a topic, use facts and definitions to develop points, and provide a concluding statement or section. **W.2.4** With guidance and support from adults, produce writing in which the development and organization are appropriate to task and purpose. **W.2.5** With guidance and support from adults and peers, focus on a topic and strengthen writing as needed by revising and editing. **W.2.7** Participate in shared research and writing projects (e.g., read a number of books on a single topic to produce a report; record science observations). **W.2.8** Recall information from experiences or gather information from provided sources to answer a question. **W.2.10** Write routinely over extended time frames (time for research, reflection, and revision) and shorter time frames (a single sitting or a day or two) for a range of discipline-specific tasks, purposes, and audiences. **SL.2.1b** Build on others' talk in conversations by linking their comments to the remarks of others. **SL.2.1c** Ask for clarification and further explanation as needed about the topics and texts under discussion. **SL.2.2** Recount or describe key ideas or details from a text read aloud or information presented orally or through other media. **SL.2.3** Ask and answer questions about what a speaker says in order to clarify comprehension, gather additional information, or deepen understanding of a topic or issue. **SL.2.6** Produce complete sentences when appropriate to task and situation in order to provide requested detail or clarification.

Next Generation Science Standards

NGSS 2-LS4-1 Make observations of plants and animals to compare the diversity of life in different habitats. **2-ESS2-2** Develop a model to represent the shapes and kinds of land and bodies of water in an area. **2-LS4-1** Make observations of plants and animals to compare the diversity of life in different habitats.

©2018 Benchmark Education Company, LLC

UNIT 4

Essential Question: **How can a story change depending on who tells it?**

ss Create a Family History Map

ELA W.2.3, W.2.4, W.2.8, W.2.10, SL.2.1a, SL.2.3

Student Objectives
I will be able to:
- Gather information about my ancestors or family and where they lived.
- Label a map to show the locations where my family lived in the past and where they live now.

Materials
Websites with printable state, country, and world maps • Printer • Colored pencils • Large sheets of construction paper

Investigate
- Remind students that in several of the stories in Unit 4 the characters traveled or moved to new locations. Ask students to talk to their family members to gather information about places their family or their ancestors have lived. Also, tell students to ask how and why they traveled to their current location.
- Ask students to bring in family photos, if possible, or ask them to print pictures of the places their families lived.

Create
- Tell students to print out country or state maps connected to their family's history. Ask them to label their map(s) to show their family's movement between locations.
- Guide students to write a short description of where their ancestors lived, when they moved, the path they took, and why they moved.
- Ask students to display their map, written description, and any visuals on a large sheet of construction paper and to add a title at the top.

Present
- Instruct students to present their maps and read aloud their description. Encourage them to display any pictures and tell about any key details or interesting information about the people and places in them.
- Encourage students to discuss the maps, listening closely to others and taking turns.

Reflect and Respond
- Ask students to reflect on the diversity of locations in which their ancestors lived and the various ways they traveled to their current location. Encourage students to look for similarities among the family histories.

ss Create a Then-and-Now Collage

ELA W.2.2, W.2.7, W.2.8, SL.2.1c, SL.2.3, SL.2.5, SL.2.6

Student Objectives
I will be able to:
- Conduct research about daily life in the past.
- Create a collage that compares and contrasts life then and now.

Materials
Internet sources that provide information about and pictures of life in the past, such as the Library of Congress • Printer • Drawing materials • Magazines • Large sheets of paper

Investigate
- Point out that several of the stories students read in Unit 4 take place in the past. Ask small groups of students to research topics related to daily life in the past. Instruct each small group to focus on one topic, such as transportation, clothing, school, children's games or activities, or forms of communication.
- Assist the small groups in using books and online sources to gather information about their topic. Ask them to find and print any pictures that will help viewers better understand what life was like in the past compared to life in the present.

Create
- Ask each group to create a collage that compares and contrasts one facet of daily life in the past and now. Students should use pictures they printed, but allow them to draw their own pictures, use pictures from magazines. Instruct students to add short labels and captions as well.
- Be sure students design their collage so that it features two distinct sections, one for the past and one for the present.
- As a group, ask students to discuss the key points they want to convey about their topic. Have them write down at least two similarities and two differences they identified.

Present
- Display the groups' collages. Invite one member from each group to explain the group's list of similarities and differences.
- Allow time for students in other groups to ask questions and clarify any information in the descriptions or the collage. Remind students to ask and answer questions using complete sentences.

Reflect and Respond
- Ask students to reflect on the information they learned and share one fact or observation that they found particularly interesting or surprising.

AR4 Grade 2 • Additional Resources   ©2018 Benchmark Education Company, LLC

Connect Across Disciplines Inquiry Projects

Keep an Ice Cube Cool

ELA W.2.2, W.2.7, SL.2.1b, NGSS 2-PS1-1, 2-PS1-2, 2-ETS1-3

Student Objectives
I will be able to:
- Investigate how to keep an object cool.
- Conduct an experiment and record data.
- Make inferences based on my findings.

Materials
Internet sites such as PBS Kids, U. S. Department of Energy, and the Lunar and Planetary Institute • Various types of insulation materials • Ice cubes • Data recording sheets • Rulers

Investigate
- Remind students that in "Wind and Sun," the man took off his coat to cool off. Tell students they will investigate the best way to stay cool by experimenting with an ice cube.
- Have small groups of students conduct Internet research to find out what happens when an ice cube is left outside in the sun. Ask them to take notes about what happens and why. Have students look for information about materials that provide insulation and keep objects cool.

Create
- Instruct groups to design and build a container that will keep an ice cube from melting in the sun—or at least slow down the process. Students should use the information they gathered from their research to help them design the container.
- Invite groups to place an ice cube inside their container and then set it outside. Every 10 to 15 minutes, ask students to inspect their ice cube and observe how much it has melted. Provide recording sheets for them to enter the data.
- At the end of the experiment, encourage group members to discuss their findings and draw conclusions about their container and the insulation material they used. Ask them to use their data to create a graph.

Present
- Have groups present their graph and explain their findings. Ask them what conclusions they drew based on the results of their experiment.
- Encourage students to discuss the experiment and the results. Guide students to link their comments to the feedback of others.

Reflect and Respond
- Based on the findings of all the groups, ask students to infer what people might use or do to keep cool on a warm day.

Useful Resources
Life Long Ago by Janine Scott
Long Ago and Today by John Serrano
School Then and Now by Robin Nelson
Transportation Then and Now by Robin Nelson

CCSS for English Language Arts

ELA W.2.2 Write informative/explanatory texts in which they introduce a topic, use facts and definitions to develop points, and provide a concluding statement or section. **W.2.3** Write narratives in which they recount a well-elaborated event or short sequence of events, include details to describe actions, thoughts, and feelings, use temporal words to signal event order, and provide a sense of closure. **W.2.4** With guidance and support from adults, produce writing in which the development and organization are appropriate to task and purpose. **W.2.7** Participate in shared research and writing projects (e.g., read a number of books on a single topic to produce a report; record science observations). **W.2.8** Recall information from experiences or gather information from provided sources to answer a question. **W.2.10** Write routinely over extended time frames (time for research, reflection, and revision) and shorter time frames (a single sitting or a day or two) for a range of discipline-specific tasks, purposes, and audiences. **SL.2.1a** Follow agreed-upon rules for discussions (e.g., gaining the floor in respectful ways listening to others with care, speaking one at a time about the topics and texts under discussion). **SL.2.1b** Build on others' talk in conversations by linking their comments to the remarks of others. **SL.2.1c** Ask for clarification and further explanation as needed about the topics and texts under discussion. **SL.2.3** Ask and answer questions about what a speaker says in order to clarify comprehension, gather additional information, or deepen understanding of a topic or issue. **SL.2.4a** Plan and deliver a narrative presentation that: recounts a well-elaborated event, includes details, reflects a logical sequence, and provides a conclusion. **SL.2.5** Create audio recordings of stories or poems; add drawings or other visual displays to stories or recounts of experiences when appropriate to clarify ideas, thoughts, and feelings. **SL.2.6** Produce complete sentences when appropriate to task and situation in order to provide requested detail or clarification.

Next Generation Science Standards

NGSS 2-PS1-1 Plan and conduct an investigation to describe and classify different kinds of materials by their observable properties. **2-PS1-2** Analyze data obtained from testing different materials to determine which materials have the properties that are best suited for an intended purpose. **2-ETS1-3** Analyze data from tests of two objects designed to solve the same problem to compare the strengths and weaknesses of how each performs.

Preteach/Reteach Routines

Table of Contents

Retelling Routine AR7

Phonological Awareness Routine. AR8

Spelling-Sound Correspondences Routine. AR9

Blending Routine AR10

Word Building Routine AR11

High-Frequency Word Routine AR12

Vocabulary Routine: Define/Example/Ask AR13

Academic Vocabulary AR14

Fluency Routine AR15

Reading Multisyllabic Words Routine. AR16

Spelling Routine. AR17

AR6   Additional Resources

©2018 Benchmark Education Company, LLC

Retelling Routine

Retelling requires students to remember as much as they can about what they read or heard. The ability to retell is a critical early reading skill and connected to the development of higher order thinking skills. It is a precursor to summarizing. Model retelling, then provide weekly practice with read-alouds or student texts.

STEP 1: Read Aloud

Display a book or read-aloud. Activate prior knowledge using the cover, title, and a few illustrations/photos in the book. Read aloud the book. Ask students to listen carefully and "remember as much as possible."

STEP 2: Prompt Retelling and Record

Ask questions to prompt student retellings. Ask questions such as: *What happened (did you find out) first? What happened (did you learn) next? Can you tell me more?* Record students' retellings on the board or chart paper.

STEP 3: Reread and Revise

Prompt students to add to their retellings. Model look-backs and/or reread the text. Ask students to listen for anything they left out of their retellings. Use their responses to add to the retelling you recorded on the board or chart paper.

STEP 4: Connect to Lives

Encourage students to make personal and across-text connections to the text. Model an example, such as how the information in a nonfiction text connects to facts you read in another text on the topic or how a fiction story connects to something that happened in your life.

Teacher Tips

- Retelling is a great partner activity and increases students' use of new language. Prompt students to retell the selection to a partner before you record class retellings.

- Provide engaging ways to retell. For example, draw a story path on a large sheet of paper. Mark the sheet beginning, middle, and end. Have students draw pictures to remind them of key events in each part of the story. Then have students "walk the story" by walking the story path and using the pictures to aid in retelling.

- Have students write key words and facts when listening to or reading a nonfiction text. They can use the words and facts in their retellings.

©2018 Benchmark Education Company, LLC

Preteach/Reteach Routines

Teacher Tips

• For rhyme, have students identify rhyming words before generating them.

• For oral blending, progress from larger word parts to smaller (blend syllables, blend onset/rime, blend phonemes).

• For oral segmenting, progress from larger word parts to smaller (clap syllables, segment onset/rime, segment phoneme by phoneme).

• Use letter cards when introducing phoneme manipulation tasks to help students better understand the task.

Phonological Awareness Routine
Pose Essential Question

Although there are no phonological awareness standards at Grade 2, some students will need additional work to develop their phonological awareness skills. Phonological awareness involves the ability to identify, blend, segment, and manipulate these sounds in spoken words. Key phonological awareness tasks include rhyme, phoneme isolation, phoneme categorization, oral blending, oral segmentation, and phonemic manipulation (addition, deletion, substitution).

STEP 1: Introduce

Explain to students the target phonological awareness task.

Example: (Rhyme) *We will be listening for words that rhyme. Rhyming words have the same ending sounds.*

Example: (Blending) *We will be listening to a series of sounds, then blend, or string together, the sounds to make words.*

STEP 2: Model

Model the target phonological awareness task with 2–3 examples. Clearly state the sounds. Stretch, elongate, or emphasize them, as needed.

Example: (Rhyme) *I'm going to say two words. Listen and tell me if they rhyme: **sat, mat**. Do **sat** and **mat** rhyme? [Wait for students to respond.] That's right, **sat** and **mat** rhyme because they both end in /at/. Listen: /s/ /at/, sat; /m/ /at/, mat. We hear /at/ at the end of **sat** and **mat**. So, **sat** and **mat** rhyme.*

Example: (Blending) *I'm going to say three sounds. Listen carefully. Blend, or put together, the sounds to make a word. The sounds are: /sss/ . . . /aaa/ . . . /t/. What word do you get when you put together these sounds? [Wait for students to respond.] That's right, when I put /sss/ . . . /aaa/ . . . /t/ together I get /sssaaat/, **sat**. The word is **sat**.*

STEP 3: Practice

Have students practice the target phonological awareness task using multiple examples. Do one or two with students, then have them do the remaining examples as a class.

Example: (Rhyme) *Now it's your turn. I will say two words. Tell me if they rhyme: **man/ fan, mop/top, boat/coat, sad/pin, read/seed, lick/pack**.*

Example: (Blending) *Now it's your turn. I will say a series of sounds. Put the sounds together to make a word: /s/ /a/ /d/, /m/ /o/ /p/, /l/ /i/ /p/, /r/ /u/ /n/.*

Spelling-Sound Correspondences Routine

STEP 1: Introduce

Display the frieze card for the target spelling-sound (e.g., vowel team /o͞o/card). Say the sound, then point to and name each spelling that stands for the sound. Have students repeat. Ask: *What is the sound? What letters (or spellings) stands for the sound?*

Example: *Display the Vowel Team /o͞o/ frieze card. The sound is /o͞o/. The /o͞o/ sound can be spelled many ways: oo, ui, ew, ue, u, ou, oe. What is the sound? (/o͞o/) What letters or spellings stand for the sound?*

STEP 2: Model

Point to each picture on the frieze card. Say the picture name, write it on the board, and underline the letter (or spelling) that stands for the sound. Do this for every picture and spelling you are focusing on in the lesson. Model how to sound out each word you write.

Example: *Look at the word I wrote: m-o-o-n. I see /o͞o/ spelled oo. Listen and watch as I sound out the word: /mo͞on/.*

STEP 3: Practice

Say a series of words with the target spelling-sound. Make sure the words are ones students can read and write based on the phonics skills they have been taught so far. Ask students to write each word and underline the target sound-spelling.

Example: *I am going to say some words with the /o͞o/ sound. Write each word and underline the spelling that stand for the /o͞o/ sound: spoon, fruit, threw, July, soup, shoe.*

Teacher Tips

- Review previously taught spelling-sounds frequently throughout the week to build mastery.

- Create additional activities with the frieze, letter, and picture cards to reinforce spelling-sound correspondences (e.g., matching games, concentration, timed activities, etc).

Preteach/Reteach Routines

Teacher Tips

- When time is limited for Practice, write the words on the board for students to blend instead of using letter cards.

- Select words to blend from upcoming Decodable Texts and other high-utility words containing the target sound-spellings.

- For vowel and consonant digraphs (e.g., *ch, sh, oa, ai*), write the spelling on one card.

Blending Routine

Blending is the main strategy readers use to decode, or sound out, words. When blending, students string together the sounds in a word to read it. It is a strategy that must be frequently modeled (with each new phonics skill) and applied both in isolation and in connected text.

STEP 1: Model

Select a word with the target phonics skill. Display letter cards for the word you want to model blending. Point to each letter card as you say the sound. Then blend the sounds together to make the word.

Example: Display the letter cards *s-a-t.* Then say the following:

This is the letter s. The letter s stands for the /s/ sound. This is the letter a. The letter a stands for the /a/ sound. Let's blend these two sounds together: /sssaaa/. This is the letter t. The letter t stands for the /t/ sound. Let's blend all the sounds together: /sssaaat/. The word is sat.

STEP 2: Practice

Distribute letter cards to students and have them place the letter card set for the day's blending on their desks. Make a word using the letter cards, but do not say the word. Have students repeat. Then ask students to blend the sounds to read the word. Continue with other words.

Example: Have students place the following letter cards on their desks: *a, m, s, t, p, o.* Place the letter cards *m-a-t* in order in a pocket chart. Have students repeat on their desks. Then ask them to blend the sounds to read the word *mat.*

STEP 3: Apply

Guide students through a reading of the Decodable Text focusing on the lesson's target phonics skill. Have students chorally read the story the first time through. Stop and model sounding out words students misread. Ask comprehension questions to check students' understanding. Have students reread the story a second time with partners or in small groups.

Preteach/Reteach Routines

Word Building Routine

Word building helps increase students' word awareness, improves the ability to fully analyze words, provides practice flexibly using learned sound-spellings, and aids in general reading and spelling growth.

STEP 1: Model

Display letter cards for a word containing the target phonics skill (e.g., too for /ōō/). Model how to add, replace, or delete one or more letters to make a new word. Make a series of 3–5 words.

Example: Display the letter cards for too. Then say the following:

• *Let's blend all the sounds together to read the word:* /tōō/, *too.*

• *Add **th** to the end.* [Add the letter cards **t-h** to the end of the word.] *Let's blend all the sounds to read the new word:* /tōōth/, *tooth.*

• *Replace the first t with **b**.* [Replace the letter **t** with **b**.] *Let's blend all the sounds together: /bōōth/.*

• *Remove the **h** from the end of the word.* [Remove the letter **h**.] *Let's blend all the sounds together: /bōōt/.*

STEP 2: Practice

Provide a series of words to guide student practice. Say one word at a time and the letter or letters to be added, removed, or changed. Ask students to blend and say the new word formed before moving on to the next word (e.g., *noon, moon, soon, spoon*).

Teacher Tips

• Begin with simple replacement of letters in one position of the word (e.g., beginning). Progress to replacing beginning and ending sounds, then add on medial sounds as students are able.

• Create a series of 4–8 words for student practice.

• When working with multiple spellings, create separate word series for each target spelling.

• Add in words with review sound-spellings when appropriate to build mastery.

©2018 Benchmark Education Company, LLC

Additional Resources **AR11**

Preteach/Reteach Routines

Teacher Tips

- Review last week's words using the Read/Spell/Write routine to extend practice over a two-week period. This will increase mastery.

- Add the words to a Word Wall.

- Have students record the words in their notebooks or on a separate sheet of paper to take home for review. Encourage them to write a sentence for each word. Reviewing the words in context is especially beneficial for English learners.

High-Frequency Word Routine

High-frequency words are the most common words in English. Some contain irregular spelling patterns. Others are used in stories before students learn the phonics skills needed to decode them. Therefore, these words must be taught as sight words.

STEP 1: Read

Display the high-frequency word card. Point to the word and read it aloud. Ask students to repeat after you.

Example: *This is the word **was**. What is the word?*

STEP 2: Spell

Spell each letter in the word as you point to it. Then ask students to chorally read and spell aloud the word.

Example: *The word was is spelled **w-a-s**. Spell the word as I point to each letter: **w-a-s**.*

STEP 3: Write

Write the word as you spell it aloud. Then have students write the word several times as they say each letter.

Example: *Watch as I write the word was. I will write **w-a-s**. Now you write the word was three times. Say each letter as you write the word.*

STEP 4: Apply

Have students use the word in an oral sentence.

Example: *Turn to a partner and use the word was in a sentence. You might begin your sentence with I was _____ .*

AR12   Additional Resources

©2018 Benchmark Education Company, LLC

Preteach/Reteach Routines

Vocabulary Routine: Define/Example/Ask

This routine, developed by Isabel Beck, is ideal for introducing new words to students. It provides a student-friendly definition, connects the word to students' experiences, and asks students to use the word in speaking to check understanding.

STEP 1: Define

Provide a student-friendly definition of the vocabulary word.

Example: *The word **gigantic** means "very big."*

STEP 2: Example

Provide an example sentence using the word. Use an example related to students' experiences.

Example: *A skyscraper is a gigantic building.*

STEP 3: Ask

Ask students a question that requires them to use the new word in their answer. Provide sentence frames for students needing additional support.

Example: *Name something you have seen that is gigantic. I saw a gigantic _____ .*

Teacher Tips

• Review new and previously taught words daily using the Define/Example/Ask routine and other vocabulary follow-up activities (e.g., act out, teach cognates, focus on synonyms and antonyms, semantic maps).

• In addition to introducing new words each week, teach word-learning strategies such as wide reading, using context clues, using roots and affixes to increase word consciousness, and dictionary usage.

©2018 Benchmark Education Company, LLC

Additional Resources **AR13**

Preteach/Reteach Routines

Teacher Tips

• When introducing a word, focus on correct pronunciation and point out any common spelling patterns in the word.

• Prompt students to create their own explanation of the word to share with the class.

• Have students list or state synonyms, antonyms, examples, nonexamples, and related words (by meaning or structure/spelling), and create nonlinguistic representations of the word (e.g., pictures).

Academic Vocabulary

This routine, developed by Kate Kinsella, is an alternate routine for working with new words. It is especially strong for English learners and can be used to extend vocabulary work after the initial Define/Example/Ask introduction.

STEP 1: Introduce the Word

Write the new word on the board (or display a vocabulary card) and pronounce the word. Have students repeat. Then introduce the following features of the word, as appropriate for students' level.

• Provide a student-friendly definition. (Compare *means "to show how things are the same or almost the same."*)
• Provide a synonym for the word. (*alike, similar*)
• Provide the various forms of the word. (*compare, comparison, comparing, comparative*)
• Provide word partners and/or sentences. (*compare/contrast*)

STEP 2: Verbal Practice

Talk about the word. Read a sentence frame using the word. Have students discuss several ways to complete the frame. Then have them say their favorite idea to complete the frame.

Example: *We will compare a _____ to a _____ to see how they are alike.*
When we compare two things, we _____ .

STEP 3: Written Practice

Have students use the word in writing. Do one or more of the following:

• **Collaborate** Have students work with a partner to complete sentence frames using the word.

• **Your Turn** Have students work independently to complete sentence frames.

• **Be an Academic Author** Have students work independently to write two sentences using the word. Each sentence should use a different form of the word (e.g., singular and plural, noun and verb).

• **Write an Academic Paragraph** Have students complete a cloze paragraph using various forms of the word (or write a brief paragraph).

AR14   Additional Resources

©2018 Benchmark Education Company, LLC

Preteach/Reteach Routines

Fluency Routine

In order to achieve mastery, students will need fluency instruction and practice at the sound, letter, word, and sentence level. Use one or more of the following fluency-building activities each week based on the week's skill focus.

Spelling-Sound Fluency

As a warm-up or transition activity, display a set of spelling-sound frieze cards. Use the cards for the spelling-sounds taught up to that point in the year. (As an alternative, write each spelling on an individual index card.) Display the cards one at a time as students say the spelling's sound. Repeat at varying speeds. Periodically mix the cards so students don't become overly familiar with the sequence.

Word Fluency

As a warm-up or transition activity, display a set of word cards with words containing the spelling-sounds taught up to that point in the year. Write 2-3 words for each spelling-sound taught. Display the cards one at a time as students chorally read the words. Repeat at varying speeds. Periodically mix the cards so students don't become overly familiar with the sequence.

Sentence Fluency

Have students do repeated readings of the Decodable Texts to build fluency. Repeated readings can include partner reading, independent reading (where you circulate and listen in on students), and rereadings at home. Include decodable stories from previous weeks to extend practice of previously taught phonics skills and build mastery.

Model Fluent Reading

Fluency includes a student's ability to read accurately (correct decoding), at an appropriate rate/speed, and with the proper expression/intonation. Each week, select an aspect of fluency to model, such as intonation. Model with sentences from student texts. Have students repeat. For example, model how you read sentences with different punctuation marks (e.g., raise your voice slightly at the end of a question). Read a sentence with the proper intonation and have students echo your reading.

©2018 Benchmark Education Company, LLC

Additional Resources **AR15**

Preteach/Reteach Routines

Teacher Tips

- Closed syllables end in a consonant and usually have a short vowel sound. (bas/ket)

- Open syllables end in a vowel and usually have a long vowel sound. (ti/ger)

- When a syllable ends in -le, the consonant before it and -le remain in the same syllable. (ta/ble)

- When a vowel team appears in a word (e.g., ai, ay, ea, ou, ow), the vowel team must remain in the same syllable. (rea/son)

- When an r-controlled vowel spelling appears in a word (e.g., er, ir, ur, ar, or), the r-controlled vowel spelling must remain in the same syllable. (mar/ket)

- When a word or syllable ends in e, the vowel before it and e work as a team. Therefore the two vowels must remain in the same syllable. (rep/tile)

Reading Multisyllabic Words Routine

Focus on common syllable patterns (closed, open, vowel team, consonant + le, final e, r-controlled vowel) and reliable syllabication rules (e.g., VCCV words, compound words) to help students break apart longer words to more easily read them.

STEP 1: Introduce a Syllable Type or Syllabication Rule

Teach the target syllable type or syllabication rule.

Example: When a vowel team such as *oo, ui, ew, ue, ou,* or *oe* appears in a long word, the vowel team must remain in the same syllable. This is because the two letters stand for one vowel sound. Each syllable in a word has only one vowel sound.

STEP 2: Build and Blend a Word

Model using the target syllable type or syllabication rule with a sample word. Build the word syllable by syllable, discussing each syllable and its pronunciation. Blend the syllables to read the whole word.

Example: Write the word *roof*. Point out and circle the vowel team *oo*. Add the word *top*. Point out the closed syllable. Explain to students that you divide the word between the two consonants in the middle of the word: *roof/top*. The vowel team must remain in the same syllable. Blend the syllables together to read the word.

STEP 3: Apply to Other Words

Provide a list of words containing the target syllable type or syllabication rule. Guide students to break apart the words and read them syllable-by-syllable.

Example: Have students break apart by syllables and blend the following words: *shampoo, moonlight, toothless, unglue, tuna.*

Preteach/Reteach Routines

Spelling Routine

In the early grades, spelling often lags behind reading development. Students' spelling can provide valuable assessment information as to which spelling-sounds they have mastered and their overall understanding of how words work. You can accelerate students' use of newly learned spelling-sounds in writing through dictation (guided spelling) and other spelling activities.

DAY 1: Pretest

Pretest students on the week's ten spelling words. These words focus on the week's target phonics skill. Say each spelling word and a sentence using the word. Ask students to write the word. When completed, write each word as you spell it aloud. Have students self-check their work. Prompt them to write the words they missed multiple times while spelling them aloud.

DAY 2: Closed Sort

Conduct a closed word sort using the week's spelling words. Write and display each spelling word on an index card. Ask students to read and chorally spell each word. Then guide students to sort the word, such as by spelling pattern for the target sound (e.g. *ai* and *ay* for the long a sound). Write each spelling pattern or a target word containing that spelling pattern at the top of each column of the sort. Have students place each index card in the correct column. When completed, have students read and chorally spell the words in each column. Ask students what they notice about the words in each column (e.g., the *ai* spelling never appears at the end of a word).

STEP 3: Word Clues

Connect the spelling words to meaning. For example, write clues or mini-definitions for about half of the spelling words (e.g., "a month"). Have students write the spelling word that goes with each clue (e.g., May). Challenge students to come up with clues for the other spelling words.

STEP 4: Categories

Connect the spelling words to related words to deepen understanding of their use. For example, write a series of words related to each of the spelling words (e.g., June, July, November, _____). Do this for about half of the spelling words. Read the words, and ask students to complete each category with a spelling word (e.g., May). Challenge students to create category word groups for the remaining spelling words.

STEP 5: Assess

Test students' spelling of the week's words. Say each spelling word and use it in a sentence. Have students write the complete sentence on paper. Then continue with the next word. When students are finished, collect their papers and analyze their spellings of any misspelled words. Use these results to plan small-group differentiated instruction and practice.

Teacher Tips

- For multisyllabic words, have students say each word syllable by syllable and spell one syllable at a time.

- Use dictation (segment a word sound-by-sound using Elkonin boxes and counters, then attach a spelling to each sound) for students who struggle spelling one-syllable words.

- Check students' writing for spelling mastery and additional words you might wish to add to their weekly spelling lists (e.g., words frequently used, but commonly misspelled).

©2018 Benchmark Education Company, LLC

Additional Resources **AR17**

Small-Group Texts for Reteaching Strategies and Skills

Title	Unit	Lexile Level	Number Level	Letter Level	Topic	Text Type/ Genre	First Reading Focus
The Power to Vote	1	260L	10	F	Government at Work	Informational Text: Social Studies	Identify Main Topic and Retell Key Details (RI.2.2)
All Work, No Play	1	400L	11	G	Government at Work	Informational Text: Social Studies	Identify Main Topic and Retell Key Details (RI.2.2)
My Mom, Our Mayor	1	430L	13	H	Government at Work	Narrative Nonfiction: Social Studies	Retell Key Details (RI.2.2)
Enforcing Rules	1	490L	28	M	Government at Work	Informational Text: Social Studies	Identify Main Topic and Retell Key Details (RI.2.2)
Alice's Trial	1	500L	24	L	Government at Work	Literary Text: Fantasy	Retell Key Details (RL.2.2)
Who Makes the Rules?	1	530L	18	J	Government at Work	Informational Text: Social Studies	Identify Main Topic and Retell Key Details (RI.2.2)
The Job of the President of the USA	1	780L	24	L	Government at Work	Informational Text: Social Studies	Retell Key Details (RI.2.2)
Dolley Madison Saves George Washington	2	310L	13	H	Characters Facing Challenges	Literary Text: Historical Fiction	Retell Key Story Details (RL.2.2)
Pinocchio	2	350L	20	K	Characters Facing Challenges	Literary Text: Fairy Tale	Retell Key Story Details (RL.2.2)
John Henry	2	350L		K	Characters Facing Challenges	Literary Text: Tall Tale	Retell Key Details (RL.2.2)
Turkey Girl	2	390L	14	H	Characters Facing Challenges	Literary Text: Folktale	Retell Key Story Details (RL.2.2)
Pandora's Box	2	390L	15	I	Characters Facing Challenges	Literary Text: Myth	Retell Key Story Details (RL.2.2)
Brer Rabbit Hears a Noise	2	420L	18	J	Characters Facing Challenges	Literary Text: Folktale	Retell Key Story Details (RL.2.2)
Arachne the Weaver	2	430L	18	J	Characters Facing Challenges	Literary Text: Myth	Retell Key Story Details (RL.2.2)
How Chipmunk Got Its Stripes	3	300L	20	K	Plants and Animals in Their Habitats	Literary Text: Folktale	Retell Key Details (RL.2.2)
Food in the Forest	3	310L	9	F	Plants and Animals in Their Habitats	Informational Text: Science	Identify Main Topic and Retell Key Details (RI.2.2)
The Ants Have a Picnic	3	370L	9	F	Plants and Animals in Their Habitats	Literary Text: Fantasy	Retell Key Story Details (RL.2.2)
My First Aquarium	3	380L	10	F	Plants and Animals in Their Habitats	Narrative Nonfiction: Science	Retell Key Details (RI.2.2)
Living in Joshua Tree	3	390L	10	F	Plants and Animals in Their Habitats	Informational Text: Science	Identify Main Topic and Retell Key Details (RI.2.2)

Small-Group Texts for Reteaching Strategies and Skills

Close Reading 1	Close Reading 2	Close Reading 4
Use Text Evidence to Draw Inferences from the Text (RI.2.6)	Use Text Features to Locate Information (RI.2.5)	Use Frequently Occurring Inflections as a Clue to the Meaning of an Unknown Word (RI.2.4, L.2.4)
Ask and Answer Questions About Key Details in a Text (RI.2.2)	Describe the Connection Between a Series of Historical Events (RI.2.2)	Use Sentence-Level Context as a Clue to the Meaning of a Word (RI.2.4, L.2.4a)
Ask and Answer Questions About Key Details (RI.2.1)	Identify an Author's Reasons to Support a Point (RI.2.8)	Use Sentence-Level Context as a Clue to the Meaning of Words (RI.2.4, L.2.4a)
Use Text Evidence to Draw Inferences from the Text (RI.2.1)	Identify the Main Purpose of a Text (What the Author Wants to Answer, Explain, or Describe) (RI.2.6)	Use the Meaning of Individual Words to Predict the Meaning of Compound Words (RI.2.4, L.2.4d)
Describe How Characters Respond to Events in a Story (RL.2.3)	Recognize Different Characters' Points of View (RL.2.5)	Use Sentence-Level Context as a Clue to the Meaning of a Word (L.2.4a)
Describe Connections in a Text (RI.2.2)	Ask and Answer Questions to Demonstrate Understanding of Key Details (RI.2.3)	Use Glossaries to Determine or Clarify the Meaning of Words (RI.2.4, L.2.4e)
Explain How a Specific Graphic Feature Contributes (RI.2.7)	Identify the Main Purpose of a Text (RI.2.6)	Use Glossaries and Beginning Dictionaries (RI.2.4, L.2.4e)
Describe Major Story Events Using Key Details (RL.2.3)	Integrate Information from Text and Illustrations to Understand Story Elements (RL.2.7)	Distinguish Shades of Meaning Among Closely Related Verbs (RL.2.4, L.2.5b)
Describe Characters in a Story Using Key Details (RL.2.3)	Use Text Evidence to Ask and Answer Questions (RL.2.1)	Distinguish Shades of Meaning Among Closely Related Verbs (RL.2.4, L.2.5b)
Recognize Different Characters' Points of View (RL.2.6)	Integrate Information from Text and Illustrations (RL.2.7)	Use Sentence-Level Context as a Clue to the Meaning of Words (RL.2.4, L.2.4a)
Describe the Characters, Setting, and Major Story Events Using Key Details (RL.2.3)	Use Key Details to Determine the Central Message, Theme, or Lesson (RL.2.2)	Use Frequently Occurring Inflections and Affixes as a Clue to the Meaning of an Unknown Word (RL.2.4, L.2.4)
Describe Characters in a Story (RL.2.3)	Determine the Central Message, Lesson, or Moral of a Story (RL.2.2)	Use Sentence-Level Context as a Clue to the Meaning of a Word (RL.2.4, L.2.4a)
Describe How Characters Respond to Events in a Story (RL.2.3)	Describe the Structure of a Story (RL.2.5)	Use Sentence-Level Context as a Clue to the Meaning of a Word (RL.2.4, L.2.4a)
Describe How Characters Respond to Events in a Story (RL.2.3)	Use Text Evidence to Ask and Answer Questions (RL.2.1)	Use a Known Root Word as a Clue to the Meaning of an Unknown Word with the Same Root (RL.2.4, L.2.4c)
Describe How Characters Respond to Events (RL.2.3)	Use Key Details to Determine the Central Message (RL.2.1, RL.2.2)	Use the Meaning of Individual Words to Predict (RL.2.4)
Identify and Describe a Sequence of Events (RI.2.3)	Determine Text Importance to Identify Main Topic and Supporting Details (RI.2.6)	Identify Frequently Occurring Root Words and Their Inflectional Forms (RI.2.4, L.2.4)
Ask Questions to Retell or Summarize (RL.2.2)	Describe Major Story Events Using Key Details (RL.2.3)	Use Sentence-Level Context as a Clue to the Meaning of a Word or Phrase (RL.2.4, L.2.4a)
Describe Steps in a Technical Procedure (RI.2.3)	Identify the Main Purpose of a Text (RI.2.6)	Use Sentence-Level Context as a Clue to the Meaning of a Word or Phrase (RI.2.4, L.2.4a)
Retell Key Details of a Text That Support a Main Idea (RI.2.2)	Identify and Describe Comparisons and Contrasts (RI.2.8)	Define Words by Category and Attribute (RI.2.4, L.2.5)

Small-Group Texts for Reteaching Strategies and Skills

Title	Unit	Number Level	Number Level	Letter Level	Topic	Text Type/ Genre	First Reading Focus
Plants and Animals in Different Seasons	3	440L	18	J	Plants and Animals in Their Habitats	Informational Text: Science	Identify Main Topic and Retell Key Details (RI.2.2)
Polar Habitats	3	510L	28	M	Plants and Animals in Their Habitats	Informational Text: Science	Identify Main Topic and Retell Key Details (RI.2.2)
Rapunzel	4	310L	14	H	Many Characters, Many Points of View	Literary Text: Fairy Tale	Retell Key Story Details (RL.2.2)
Cat in Boots	4	370L	13	H	Many Characters, Many Points of View	Literary Text: Fairy Tale	Retell Key Story Details (RL.2.2)
Winter Carnival	4	380L	18	J	Many Characters, Many Points of View	Literary Text: Realistic Fiction	Retell Key Story Details (RL.2.2)
The Dog and the Wolf	4	440L		N	Many Characters, Many Points of View	Literary Text: Fable	Retell Key Details (RL.2.2)
The Three Billy Goats Gruff	4	500L	16	I	Many Characters, Many Points of View	Literary Text: Fairy Tale	Retell Key Story Details (RL.2.2)
Horseshoe Soup	4	530L	18	J	Many Characters, Many Points of View	Literary Text: Variant Tale	Retell Key Story Details (RL.2.2)
Laura's Story	4	540L	24	L	Many Characters, Many Points of View	Narrative Nonfiction: Social Studies	Retell Key Story Details (RI.2.2)
Push, Pull, Lift!	5	350L	16	I	Solving Problems through Technology	Informational Text: Science	Identify Main Topic and Retell Key Details (RI.2.2)
The Friendship Bridge	5	380L	20	K	Solving Problems Through Technology	Literary Text: Fable	Retell Key Story Details (RL.2.2)
Simple Machines	5	500L	20	K	Solving Problems Through Technology	Informational Text: Science	Identify Main Topic and Retell Key Details (RI.2.2)
Jenner and Fleming: Two Heroes of Medicine	5	520L	15	I	Solving Problems Through Technology	Informational Text: Science Biography	Retell Key Details (RI.2.2)
Bridges	5	590L	20	K	Solving Problems Through Technology	Informational Text: Science	Identify Main Topic and Retell Key Details (RI.2.2)
George Washington Carver	5	600L	15	I	Solving Problems Through Technology	Informational Text: Science Biography	Identify Main Topic and Retell Key Details (RI.2.2)
Taking Photographs	5	750L	28	M	Solving Problems Through Technology	Informational Text: Procedural	Identify Main Topic and Retell Key Details (RI.2.2)
The Prince and the Pauper	6	200L	18	J	Tales to Live By	Literary Text: Fantasy	Retell Key Story Details (RL.2.2)
The Lion and the Mouse	6	300L		J	Tales to Live By	Literary Text: Fable	Retell Key Details (RL.2.2)
Androcles and the Lion	6	340L	20	K	Tales to Live By	Literary Text: Fable	Retell Key Story Details (RL.2.2)

Small-Group Texts for Reteaching Strategies and Skills

Close Reading 1	Close Reading 2	Close Reading 4
Use Text Evidence to Draw Inferences from the Text (RI.2.1)	Explain How a Specific Graphic Feature Contributes to and Clarifies a Text (RI.2.7)	Use a Known Root Word as a Clue to the Meaning of an Unknown Word with the Same Root (RI.2.4, L.2.4c)
Identify and Describe Comparisons and Contrasts (RI.2.3)	Identify the Main Purpose of a Text (RI.2.6)	Distinguish Shades of Meaning Among Closely Related Adjectives (RI.2.4, L.2.5b)
Describe Characters in a Story (RL.2.3)	Integrate Information from Text and Illustrations to Understand Story Elements (RL.2.7)	Use Sentence-Level Context as a Clue to the Meaning of a Phrase (RL.2.4, L.2.4a)
Describe Story Structure (RL.2.5)	Use Text Evidence to Ask and Answer Questions (RL.2.1)	Use a Known Root Word as a Clue to the Meaning of an Unknown Word with the Same Root (RL.2.4, L.2.4c)
Use Information From Illustrations and Words to Demonstrate Understanding of Setting and Plot (RL.2.7)	Describe the Structure of a Story (RL.2.5)	Use the Meaning of Individual Words to Predict the Meaning of Compound Words (RL.2.4, L.2.4d)
Use Text Evidence to Draw Inferences (RI.2.1)	Use Key Details to Determine the Central Message (RL.2.1, RL.2.2)	Use Sentence-Level Context as a Clue to the Meaning of Words (RL.2.4, L.2.4a)
Use Information from the Illustrations and Words to Understand the Setting (RL.2.7)	Use Text Evidence to Ask and Answer Questions (RL.2.1)	Use Words and Phrases Acquired Through Conversations, Reading and Being Read To, and Responding to Texts (RL.2.4, L.2.6)
Describe How Characters Respond to Events in a Story (RL.2.3)	Describe the Structure of a Story (RL.2.5)	Identify Real-Life Connections Between Words and Their Use (RL.2.4, L.2.5a)
Identify and Describe a Sequence of Events (RI.2.3)	Identify the Author's Point of View (RI.2.6)	Determine the Meaning of the New Word When a Known Prefix is Added to a Known Word (RI.2.4, L.2.4b)
Integrate Information from Text and Illustrations to Understand Key Details (RI.2.7)	Determine Main Topic and Key Supporting Details (RI.2.2)	Use Words and Phrases Acquired Through Conversations, Reading and Being Read To, and Responding to Texts (RI.2.4, L.2.6)
Describe How Characters Respond to Events in a Story (RL.2.3)	Ask and Answer Questions to Determine Key Details (RL.2.1)	Use a Known Root Word to Determine Meaning (RL.2.4, L.2.4c)
Identify the Main Purpose of a Text (RI.2.6)	Use Text Features to Locate Information (RI.2.5)	Use Sentence-Level Context as a Clue to the Meaning of a Word (RI.2.4, L.2.4a)
Use Text Features to Locate Information (RI.2.5)	Identify and Describe Comparisons and Contrasts (RI.2.3)	Use Sentence-Level Context as a Clue to the Meaning of Words (L.2.4a)
Identify Focus of Specific Paragraphs (RI.2.2)	Identify the Author's Main Purpose in a Text (RI.2.6)	Use Glossaries and Beginning Dictionaries to Determine or Clarify the Meaning of Words and Phrases (RI.2.4, L.2.4e)
Ask and Answer Questions to Demonstrate Understanding of Key Details (RI.2.1)	Identify the Main Purpose of a Text (RI.2.6)	Use Sentence-Level Context as a Clue to the Meaning of a Phrase (RI.2.4, L.2.4a)
Identify and Describe Steps in a Process (RI.2.3)	Explain How a Specific Graphic Feature Contributes to and Clarifies a Text (RI.2.7)	Use a Known Root Word as a Clue to the Meaning of an Unknown Word with the Same Root (RI.2.4, L.2.4c)
Describe the Settings in a Story (RL.2.3)	Use Text Evidence to Draw Inferences from a Text (RL.2.1)	Use Beginning Dictionaries to Determine or Clarify the Meanings of Words (RL.2.4, L.2.4e)
Describe How Characters Respond to Events in a Story (RL.2.3)	Use Key Details to Determine the Central Message, Theme, or Lesson (RL.2.2)	Use a Known Root Word as a Clue to the Meaning of an Unknown Word With the Same Root (RL.2.4, L.2.4c)
Describe How Characters Respond to Events in a Story (RL.2.3)	Recognize Different Characters' Points of View (RL.2.6)	Use Sentence-Level Context as a Clue to the Meaning of a Word or Phrase (RL.2.4, L.2.4a)

©2018 Benchmark Education Company, LLC

Small-Group Texts for Reteaching Strategies and Skills

Title	Unit	Number Level	Number Level	Letter Level	Theme	Text Type/ Genre	First Reading Focus
How the Turtle Cracked Its Shell	6	430L	15	I	Tales to Live By	Literary Text: Folktale	Retell Key Story Details (RL.2.2)
The Bremen Town Musicians	6	430L	24	L	Tales to Live By	Literary Text: Fairy Tale	Retell Key Story Details (RL.2.2)
Why Mosquitoes Buzz in People's Ears	6	500L	28	M	Tales to Live By	Literary Text: Folktale	Retell Key Story Details (RL.2.2)
The Three Little Pigs	6	600L	13	H	Tales to Live By	Literary Text: Fairy Tale	Retell Key Story Details (RL.2.2)
In My Opinion…George Catlin Was a Great Painter	7	480L	18	J	Investigating the Past	Opinion Text	Identify Main Topic and Retell Key Details (RI.2.2)
Finding Fossils	7	500L	15	I	Investigating the Past	Informational Text: Science	Identify Main Topic and Retell Key Details (RI.2.2)
A Bowl of Dust	7	500L	18	J	Investigating the Past	Literary Text: Historical Fiction	Retell Key Details (RL.2.2)
Charlie's Museum Adventure	7	590L	15	I	Investigating the Past	Literary Text: Fantasy	Retell Key Story Details (RL.2.2)
William's Journal	7	590L	24	L	Investigating the Past	Literary Text: Historical Fiction	Retell Key Story Details (RL.2.2)
The Underground Railroad	7	590L	24	L	Investigating the Past	Informational Text: Social Studies	Identify Main Topic and Retell Key Details (RI.2.2)
Getting Around the Wild West	7	670L	18	J	Investigating the Past	Informational Text: Social Studies	Identify Main Topic and Retell Key Details (RI.2.2)
Paul Bunyan	8	400L		J	Wind and Water Change Earth	Literary Text: Tall Tale	Retell Key Details (RL.2.2)
Earth's Surface	8	480L	14	H	Wind and Water Change Earth	Informational Text: Science	Identify Main Topic and Retell Key Details (RI.2.2)
Neptune and Minerva	8	500L		M	Wind and Water Change Earth	Literary Text: Myth	Retell Key Details (RL.2.2)
Mountains	8	520L	20	K	Wind and Water Change Earth	Informational Text: Science	Identify Main Topic and Retell Key Details (RI.2.2)
Erosion	8	590L	18	J	Wind and Water Change Earth	Informational Text: Science	Identify Main Topic and Retell Key Details (RI.2.2)
Let's Look at the Dinosaurs	8	620L	11	G	Wind and Water Change Earth	Informational Text: Social Studies	Identify Main Topic and Retell Key Details (RI.2.2)
Twisters	8	760L	24	L	Wind and Water Change Earth	Informational Text: Science	Identify Main Topic and Retell Key Details (RI.2.2)
Supply and Demand	9	290L	20	K	Buyers and Sellers	Informational Text: Social Studies	Identify Main Topic and Retell Key Details (RI.2.2)

AR22   Additional Resources

Small-Group Texts for Reteaching Strategies and Skills

Close Reading 1	Close Reading 2	Close Reading 4
Describe Characters in a Story (RL.2.3)	Use Text Evidence to Draw Inferences from a Text (RL.2.1)	Use Sentence-Level Context as a Clue to the Meaning of a Phrase (RL.2.4, L.2.4a)
Describe Characters in a Story Using Key Details (RL.2.3)	Integrate Information from Text and Illustrations to Understand Story Elements (RL.2.7)	Use a Known Root Word as a Clue to the Meaning of an Unknown Word with the Same Root (RL.2.4, L.2.4c)
Identify the Setting in a Story (RL.2.3)	Acknowledge Differences in Characters' Points of View (RL.2.6)	Use Words and Phrases Acquired Through Conversations, Reading and Being Read To, and Responding to Texts (RL.2.4, L.2.6)
Describe Characters in a Story (RL.2.3)	Use Text Evidence to Ask and Answer Questions (RL.2.1)	Identify Real-Life Connections Between Words and Their Uses (RL.2.4, L.2.5a)
Describe How Reasons Support Specific Points the Author Makes in a Text (RI.2.8)	Explain How a Specific Graphic Feature Contributes to and Clarifies a Text (RI.2.7)	Distinguish Shades of Meaning Among Closely Related Adjectives (RI.2.4, L.2.5b)
Ask and Answer Questions About Key Details in a Text (RI.2.1)	Use Text Features to Locate Key Facts or Information (RI.2.5)	Use Sentence-Level Context as a Clue to the Meaning of a Word or Phrase (RL.2.4, L.2.4a)
Integrate Information from Text and Illustrations (RL.2.7)	Use Text Evidence to Ask and Answer Questions (RL.2.1)	Use the Meaning of Individual Words to Predict the Meaning of Compound Words (L.2.4d)
Integrate Information from Text and Illustrations to Understand Story Elements (RL.2.7)	Recognize Different Characters' Points of View (RL.2.6)	Use Sentence-Level Context as a Clue to the Meaning of a Word (RL.2.4, L.2.4a)
Describe Characters in a Story Using Key Details (RL.2.3)	Describe the Structure of a Story (RL.2.5)	Identify Real-Life Connections Between Words and Their Uses (RL.2.4, L.2.5a)
Identify and Describe Causes and Effects (RI.2.3)	Explain How a Specific Graphic Feature Contributes to and Clarifies a Text (RI.2.7)	Use a Known Root Word as a Clue to the Meaning of an Unknown Word with the Same Root (RI.2.4, L.2.4c)
Identify the Main Purpose of a Text (RI.2.6)	Know and Use Various Text Features to Locate Key Facts or Information (RI.2.5)	Use Glossaries and Beginning Dictionaries to Determine or Clarify Meaning (RI.2.4, L.2.4e)
Describe Major Events (RL.2.3)	Integrate Information from Text and Illustrations (RL.2.7)	Use Sentence-Level Context as a Clue to the Meaning of Words (RL.2.4a, L.2.5a)
Explain How a Specific Graphic Feature Contributes to and Clarifies a Text (RI.2.7)	Identify and Describe Comparisons and Contrasts (RI.2.3)	Use Sentence-Level Context as a Clue to the Meaning of a Word or Phrase (RI.2.4, L.2.4a)
Describe the Structure of a Story (RI.2.5)	Use Information Gained From Illustrations (RI..2.3)	Use a Known Root Word As a Clue to the Meaning of an Unknown Word With the Same Root (RI..2.4, L.2.4c)
Use Graphic Features to Understand a Text (RI.2.7)	Describe Connections in a Text (RI.2.2)	Use Adjectives to Describe (RI.2.4, L.2.6)
Use Text Features to Locate Key Facts or Information (RI.2.5)	Identify and Describe Causes and Their Effects (RI.2.3)	Use Sentence-Level Context as a Clue to the Meaning of a Word (RI.2.4, L.2.4a)
Describe Connections in a Text (RI.2.3)	Explain How Specific Images Contribute to and Clarify a Text (RI.2.7)	Identify Real-Life Connections Between Words and Their Uses (RI.2.4, L.2.5a)
Identify and Describe Causes and Their Effects (RI.2.3)	Explain How a Specific Graphic Feature Contributes to and Clarifies a Text (RI.2.7)	Use Glossaries to Determine or Clarify the Meaning of Words (RI.2.4, L.2.4e)
Identify and Describe Causes and Their Effects (RI.2.3)	Use Text Evidence to Draw Inferences from the Text (RI.2.1)	Distinguish Shades of Meaning Among Closely Related Verbs (RI.2.4, L.2.5b)

Small-Group Texts for Reteaching Strategies and Skills

Title	Unit	Number Level	Number Level	Letter Level	Topic	Text Type/ Genre	First Reading Focus
A Trip to the Market	9	350L	12	G	Buyers and Sellers	Literary Text: Realistic Fiction	Retell Key Story Details (RL.2.2)
People Work in Our Community	9	360L	11	G	Buyers and Sellers	Informational Text: Social Studies	Identify Main Topic and Retell Key Details (RI.2.2)
Simple Simon Is Silly!	9	390L	12	G	Buyers and Sellers	Opinion Text	Identify Main Topic and Retell Key Details (RI.2.2)
The Cost of Dinner	9	430L	28	M	Buyers and Sellers	Informational Text: Social Studies	Identify Main Topic and Retell Key Details (RI.2.2)
Simple Simon	9	520L		H	Buyers and Sellers	Literary Text: Fantasy	Retell Key Details (RL.2.2)
Where Does Food Come From?	9	820L	28	M	Buyers and Sellers	Informational Text: Social Studies	Retell Key Details (RI.2.2)
What Is Matter?	10	380L	18	J	States of Matter	Informational Text: Science	Identify Main Topic and Retell Key Details (RI.2.2)
Water All Around	10	410L	10	F	States of Matter	Informational Text: Science	Identify Main Topic and Retell Key Details (RI.2.2)
The States of Matter	10	420L	14	H	States of Matter	Informational Text: Science	Identify the Main Topic and Retell Key Details (RI.2.2)
Maggie Makes Macaroni	10	430L	14	H	States of Matter	Literary Text: Realistic Fiction	Retell Key Story Details (RL.2.2)
The States of Matter	10	490L		I	States of Matter	Informational Text: Science	Identify Main Topic and Retell Key Details (RI.2.2)
Measure Up!	10	560L	13	H	States of Matter	Informational Text: Science	Identify Main Topic and Retell Key Details (RI.2.2, RI.2.3)
Four Faces in Rock	10	720L	18	J	States of Matter	Informational Text: Social Studies	Identify Main Topic and Retell Key Details (RI.2.2)

Small-Group Texts for Reteaching Strategies and Skills

Close Reading 1	Close Reading 2	Close Reading 4
Describe How Characters Respond to Events in a Story (RL.2.3)	Integrate Information from Text and Illustrations to Understand Story Elements (RL.2.7)	Use Sentence-Level Context as a Clue to the Meaning of a Word (RL.2.4, L.2.4a)
Determine the Main Topic and Key Supporting Details (RI.2.2)	Ask Questions to Integrate and Evaluate Multiple Sources of Information (RI.2.1)	Use a Known Root Word as a Clue to the Meaning of an Unknown Word with the Same Root (RI.2.4, L.2.4c)
Identify an Author's Reasons to Support a Point (RI.2.8)	Ask and Answer Questions About Key Details in a Text (RI.2.1)	Use Sentence-Level Context as a Clue to the Meaning of a Word (RI.2.4, L.2.4a)
Use Text Evidence to Draw Inferences from the Text (RI.2.1)	Identify and Describe Comparisons and Contrasts (RI.2.3)	Identify Real-Life Connections Between Word and Their Uses (RI.2.4, L.2.5a)
Describe How Characters Respond to Events (RL.2.3)	Use Text Evidence to Make Inferences (RL.2.1)	Identify Real-Life Connections Between Words and Their Use (RL.2.4, L.2.5a)
Use Text Features to Locate Information (RI.2.7)	Explain How a Specific Graphic Feature Contributes (RI.2.7)	Use Sentence-Level Context as a Clue to the Meaning of Words (L.2.4a)
Identify and Describe Comparisons and Contrasts (RI.2.3)	Use Text Features to Locate Information (RI.2.5)	Use Sentence-Level Context as a Clue to the Meaning of a Word (RI.2.4, L.2.4a)
Explain How Specific Images Contribute to and Clarify a Text (RI.2.7)	Identify and Describe Comparisons and Contrasts (RI.2.3)	Use Beginning Dictionaries to Determine or Clarify the Meaning of Words (RI.2.4, L.2.4e)
Ask and Answer Questions to Demonstrate Understanding of Key Details in a Text (RI.2.1)	Describe Connections in a Text (RI.2.4)	Use a Known Root Word as a Clue to the Meaning of an Unknown Word with the Same Root (RI.2.4, L.2.4c)
Describe How Characters Respond to Events in a Story (RL.2.3)	Describe the Structure of a Story (RL.2.5)	Use Sentence-Level Context as a Clue to the Meaning of a Word (RL.2.4, L.2.4a)
Use Text Features to Locate Information (RI.2.5)	Ask and Answer Questions About Key Details in a Text (RI.2.1)	Distinguish Shades of Meaning Among Closely Related Verbs (RI.2.4, L.2.5b)
Ask and Answer Questions About Key Details in a Text (RI.2.1)	Use Text Features to Locate Key Facts or Information (RI.2.5)	Use Sentence-Level Context as a Clue to the Meaning of a Word (RL.2.4, L.2.4a)
Use Text Features to Locate Key Facts or Information (RI.2.2)	Explain How a Specific Graphic Feature Contributes to and Clarifies a Text (RI.2.7)	Use a Known Root Word as a Clue to the Meaning of an Unknown Word with the Same Root (RI.2.4, L.2.4c)

©2018 Benchmark Education Company, LLC

Collaborative Conversation

Maximizing the Quality of Classroom Collaborative Conversations

by Jeff Zwiers, Ed.D.

> "The richest conversations have ideas that become clearer and stronger as students talk—such that all participating students walk away from the conversation with more insight and clarity than they had before they conversed."
>
> Jeff Zwiers

Productive classroom conversations include many features and require many skills. Fortunately, most of these features and skills can be modeled and scaffolded. The mini-lessons in your *Benchmark Advance* Teacher Resource System offer a wide range of conversational opportunities and helpful scaffolds to support rich conversations. For these conversations to be successful learning experiences, however, teachers must adapt lessons to meet the unique needs of their students. This article outlines several teacher habits, skills, and ideas for maximizing the quality of students' collaborative conversations in every unit of the program.

There are two common types of conversations that take place in the classroom. In the first, participants build up an idea together. In the second, participants discuss multiple ideas in order to choose one idea over another. An idea can take many forms: an answer to an essential question, an opinion, an inference, a hypothesis, a description of a complex process, a solution to a problem, a theme in a story, a comparison, etc.

Teachers and students can better understand how to improve conversations with the tools that accompany the *Benchmark Advance* program. The first tool, the *Conversation Blueprint*, is a visual guide to help teachers scaffold students' conversations. This tool shows the structure of the two main types of conversations that should happen during lessons.

The tools especially designed for students are the *Think-Speak-Listen Bookmarks* for grades K–1 and the *Think-Speak-Listen Flip Book* for Grades 2–6. These tools offer sentence stems for various skills within a conversation. Each bookmark focuses on a specific conversation skill. The flip book provides stems for expressing and eliciting general ideas as well as stems for clarifying, supporting, and discussing the choice of one idea over others.

Think-Speak-Listen Bookmarks and Flip Books for Students

Collaborative Conversation

Building Up an Idea Together

To support the first type of conversation, three key skills are needed: expressing an idea, clarifying the idea, and supporting the idea with reasons, evidence, examples, and explanations. First, students express an idea relevant to the conversation prompt. Then students clarify the idea by defining and explaining what they mean as they use appropriate academic terms. They can also refer to the stems in the Think-Speak-Listen tools for language structures to help them pose and clarify ideas. A vital part of building up an idea is supporting the idea with **reasons**, **evidence**, and **examples**. Usually, students need to **explain** how the reasons, evidence, and examples support the idea.

For example, at the end of Grade 1, Unit 3 (*Plants and Animals Grow and Change*), the teacher prompts students to talk about the essential question, "Why do living things change?" Students talk in small groups to build up their ideas together in preparation for writing about the topic. Before and during the conversations, the teacher reminds students to stay on topic, listen respectfully, and build on one another's comments. Here is an example.

Conversation Blueprint, side 1

Carlos:	Based on what I read, an idea that I have is that living things change because they want to live. (*Expresses an idea*)
Nina:	What do you mean? (*Asks for clarification*)
Carlos:	They change so they won't die. Like to eat and move. (*Clarifies*)
Ana:	Like the frog? Remember? It was in an egg in water so it wouldn't dry and die, then it grew a tail to swim. (*Supports Carlos's idea with an example*)
David:	Yeah, with no tail it dies cuz it can't eat. But then it loses its tail. (*Adds clarity to the example*)
Nina:	Why? (*Connects back to prompt; clarifies*)
David:	Maybe so it can jump better. To get away from snakes.
Ana:	I hate snakes.
Carlos:	So do frogs. Are we done?
Ana:	No. That's just one animal. What about another animal change? (*Asks for another example; gets back on topic*)
Nina:	Butterfly. (*Provides another example*)
David:	Why does it change to stay alive? It could just stay a caterpillar. (*Asks for clarification focused on prompt*)
Nina:	I don't think it will live long like that. Butterflies can fly to warm places and get away from birds.

Notice how the students use the skills of expressing, clarifying, and supporting to build up an idea during the conversation. These skills help them stay on topic and solidify their knowledge of how living things change.

Collaborative Conversation

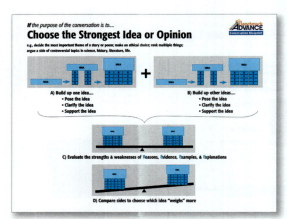

Conversation Blueprint, side 2

Choosing One Idea Over Others

The second type of conversation builds on the first type. Students first build up one idea as just described, and after it is built up, they build up a second idea, and even others, if needed. After building up two or more ideas, the students converse to decide which idea is "stronger." A good example of this type of conversation is an argument. In an argument, a person often takes a side (i.e., makes a case for one idea) and supports it to show how it outweighs the other side(s). Learning to choose one idea over others—and respectfully and effectively argue about it—is a vital skill for life, one that students should work on every year in school.

The Conversation Blueprint illustrates how to structure a rich conversation that helps participants choose one idea over another. Students must first build up one idea with clarifications, reasons, evidence, examples, and explanations. Students then build up a second idea, and so on. Only after students have clarified and built up each idea are they ready to evaluate the strengths and weaknesses of the reasons, evidence, examples, and explanations that support each idea. Evaluation means deciding how valuable, or "heavy," the support is for an idea. For example, when conversing about the prompt, "What is the most important reason to read stories?" a group of students built up two ideas: (1) we read stories to show us how to be better people; and (2) we read stories to learn about others. They came up with examples for both ideas, and in some cases the same stories were used on both sides. They found more examples for the second idea, but one student, Brenda, argued that being better people was very heavy, even if there were more examples on the other side.

Then they compared the two ideas to choose which was "heavier"—that is, which idea had more convincing evidence. Manuel said he also thought that being better people weighed more than just learning about others. "I think we need to have better people, not just people who know more stuff about others." They chose the first idea but conceded that the second idea was important, too. Indeed, this is what the teacher wanted. She didn't care what idea they ultimately chose, but she did want them to think carefully about each idea and argue each side. Also, notice that this prompt forced students to choose an idea. If it had been, "Why do we read stories?" students could have just come up with a list of reasons and not done the cognitive work of evaluating and comparing the two ideas.

Let's look at a sample conversation between two 4th grade students who were discussing the prompt, "Do earthquakes have a more positive or negative impact on our lives?" To set up the conversation, students were given time to research the positive and negative impacts of earthquakes. Again, notice how the prompt, which asked for an argument-based choice as a result of the conversation, spurred students to clarify, support, and evaluate ideas more than if they had been prompted just to describe how earthquakes impact people.

Collaborative Conversation

Daniela: What negative impacts do earthquakes have on us?

Nico: Buildings fall down. (*Expresses one idea*)

Daniela: Can you elaborate? (*Asks for clarification*)

Nico: The ground shakes and buildings fall down. People die and lose their homes and their things get all smashed up. (*Clarifies*)

Daniela: What's the evidence of that? (*Asks for support*)

Nico: For example, Emma Burke's account of the San Francisco earthquake told about the damage for that family. And it said like 80 percent of the city was destroyed. That's a lot. (*Provides evidence from a text*)

Daniela: And the fire it started. And in the news, lots of people still die in earthquakes. And earthquakes cause tsunamis that flood people. They are hard to predict. (*Adds to evidence*)

Nico: What about positive impact? Is there any?

Daniela: I read that the earthquake plates move and bring up oil and minerals that we use. That's a good impact. We need oil. (*Provides reason for positive impact and an explanation about the importance of oil*)

Nico: So is the impact more good or bad?

Daniela: I don't know. Maybe we…I don't know. Let's see how heavy each idea is.

Nico: OK, the bad impact is destruction of buildings and lots of people dying from it. And fires and floods. People dying is very heavy. (*Evaluates the "weight" of first idea*)

Daniela: And for good impacts, the plates help us get minerals and oil. We need these things for energy and cars, so it's heavy. (*Evaluates the "weight" of second idea*)

Nico: So it's like people dying on one side and minerals and oil on the other? What's heavier? (*Begins to compare weights of two ideas*)

Daniela: I think people dying. We need oil and minerals, but they aren't as important as people's lives. (*Compares ideas using the criterion of human life*)

Nico: I agree because think if it was you or your family in a falling building. You don't care about oil or minerals, just staying alive. (*Final explanation of choice*)

Students will never have this exact conversation, and no two conversations among students will ever be the same. This is what makes collaborative conversation so exciting and unpredictable. Just remember to keep the structures, features, and skills in mind. Use the tools as needed, but remember to reduce student reliance on them during the year. Build a culture in the classroom that values conversation and the ideas of others. In *Benchmark Advance*, you will find a wealth of opportunities to build such a culture, and in doing so, you will equip students with not only highly valuable knowledge and literacy skills, but also priceless abilities for communicating with other humans and work together to build up ideas that are unique and generative.

©2018 Benchmark Education Company, LLC

Conversation Blueprint

If the purpose of the conversation is to...

Build Up an Idea Together

Then...

1. Express an idea, or ask others to express one.
2. Clarify the idea, or ask others for clarification.
3. Support the idea, or ask others to support it using reasons, evidence, examples, and explanations.

R	E	E	E

Reasons
Evidence
Examples
Explanations

An idea can be many things:
- an opinion
- a hypothesis
- the theme of a story or poem
- the purpose of a text
- an explanation of how something works
- a cause or effect
- a character's motivation
- a way to solve a problem

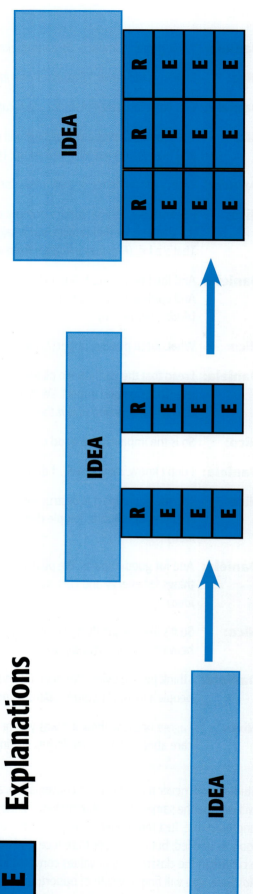

AR30 Additional Resources

©2018 Benchmark Education Company, LLC

Conversation Blueprint

If the purpose of the conversation is to...

Choose the Strongest Idea or Opinion

e.g., decide the most important theme of a story or poem; make an ethical choice; rank multiple things; argue a side of controversial topics in science, history, literature, life.

Then...

 +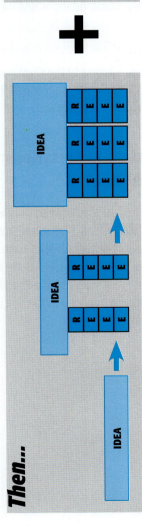

A) Build up one idea.
- Pose the idea.
- Clarify the idea.
- Support the idea.

B) Build up other ideas.
- Pose the idea.
- Clarify the idea.
- Support the idea.

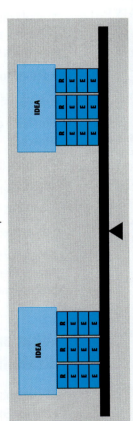

C) Evaluate the strengths and weaknesses of **Reasons**, **Evidence**, **Examples**, and **Explanations**.

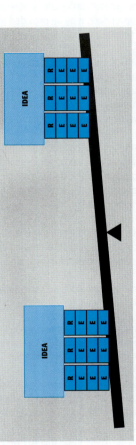

D) Compare sides to choose which idea "weighs" more.

©2018 Benchmark Education Company, LLC

Additional Resources **AR31**

Access and Equity

CCSSO Statement About the Application of the CCSS to Students with Disabilities

How these high standards are taught and assessed is of the utmost importance in reaching this diverse group of students.

Promoting a culture of high expectations for all students is a fundamental goal of the Common Core State Standards. In order to participate with success in the general curriculum, students with disabilities, as appropriate, may be provided additional supports and services, such as:

• Instructional supports for learning based on the principles of Universal Design for Learning (UDL), which foster student engagement by presenting information in multiple ways and allowing for diverse avenues of action and expression.

• Instructional accommodations (Thompson, Morse, Sharpe & Hall, 2005), changes in materials or procedures which do not change the standards but allow students to learn within the framework of the Common Core.

• Assistive technology devices and services to ensure access to the general education curriculum and the Common Core State Standards.

From the Common Core State Standards Initiative. 2010.

The California English Language Arts and English Language Development (ELA/ELD) Framework echoes these recommendations by stating:

"Most students who are eligible for special education services are able to achieve the standards when the following three conditions are met:

1. Standards are implemented within the foundational principles of Universal Design for Learning.

2. Evidence-based instructional strategies are implemented and instructional materials and curriculum reflect the interests, preferences, and readiness of each student to maximize learning potential.

3. Appropriate accommodations are provided to help students access grade-level content."

Meeting the Needs of Students with Disabilities:
The Power of Access and Equity

By Erin Marie Mason and Marjorie McCabe, Ph.D.

Benchmark Advance is designed to support you in meeting the needs of all learners through systematic, evidence-based methods which offer differentiated and scaffolded instruction for students. Each lesson offers multiple opportunities to individualize and/or customize learning through ongoing assessment and progress monitoring, flexible grouping, and scaffolding. The purpose of this article is to illuminate how these materials can assist you in providing access and equity for your students with disabilities. You will find step-by-step guidelines to support you in the collaborative process of:

• getting to know your students with disabilities as individuals;

• using the Individual Education Program (IEP) or 504 Plan;

• building collaboration between the general education teacher and special education teacher;

• utilizing the differentiation and scaffolding features of these instructional materials;

• implementing appropriate and effective accommodations and modifications to enhance learning; and

• providing culturally and linguistically responsive instruction and accommodations.

Benchmark Advance will help you maximize access to the Common Core and elevate engagement for students with disabilities by guiding you through the instructional planning process and by directing you to recommended resources.

What are the national and state expectations for students with disabilities and the Common Core?

All students, including students with disabilities, are required to have access to the Common Core for English Language Arts and English Language Development. There are national and state recommendations for ensuring students with disabilities have appropriate access to the Common Core. In fact, the Common Core State Standards include a section on how to best provide appropriate access to the standards for student with disabilities, entitled Application to Students with Disabilities. Key elements are provided in the box on left.

AR32 Additional Resources

©2018 Benchmark Education Company, LLC

Access and Equity

How/where can I learn more about the types of disabilities of my students?

In alignment with the federal Individuals with Disabilities Education Improvement Act (IDEIA), reauthorized in 2004, California schools provide special education and other related services as a part of a guaranteed free appropriate public education to students who qualify under one of the following categories (presented alphabetically): autism, deafness, deaf-blindness, emotional disturbance, hearing impairment, intellectual disability, multiple disabilities, orthopedic impairment, other health impairment, specific learning disability, speech or language impairment, traumatic brain injury, or visual impairment, including blindness.

However, approximately two-thirds of the students in special education qualify under speech and language impairment or specific learning disabilities (California Department of Education, Data Quest, 2011). Furthermore, the area of literacy is the area most affected by learning disabilities. The goals and objectives addressed in many IEPs are very often in reading and written expression.

Create safe, respectful, and stimulating learning environments for all students, including students with disabilities.

According to the California Framework, "…some groups of students experience a low level of safety and acceptance in schools for reasons including cultural, ethnic, and linguistic background; disability; sexual orientation; economic; and other factors. Students must be provided . . . settings that are physically and psychologically safe, respectful, and intellectually stimulating."

The first step in helping students with disabilities to achieve their highest potential is to address the learning environment to make sure it is physically and psychologically safe, respectful and intellectually stimulating. Without this foundation in place, students will not be able to focus on academic instruction. All students need to feel safe, respected, and welcomed in school. Students with disabilities will not be successful if they are anxious or intimidated. The California Framework emphasizes this point.

The teacher must build a culture of valuing individual differences (in learning, culture, ethnicity, language, etc). Model inclusive language and behavior. Discuss and role play situations that make students with disabilities feel included, as well as situations that may be offensive to students with disabilities. Educate all students about the types of disabilities of classmates. Have zero tolerance for any type of teasing or bullying. Reinforce the value of individual differences.

Recommended Resource:

For more information on these disabilities, refer to the National Dissemination Center for Children with Disabilities http://nichcy.org/disability/categories.

Application to Students with Disabilities, http://www.corestandards.org/assets/application-to-students-with-disabilities.pdf.

©2018 Benchmark Education Company, LLC

Access and Equity

Recommended Resource:

Individualized Education Program (IEP) http://www.ncld.org/learning-disability-resources/videos/video-what-is-an-iep

504 plan http://specialchildren.about.com/od/504s/qt/sample504.htm

How do I plan, deliver, and assess instruction for the students with disabilities in my class?

1. Get to know your students with disabilities as individuals.

Students with disabilities represent the full range of diversity regarding culture, language, socioeconomic background, sexual orientation, age, gender, and more, and they are simultaneously members of these multiple demographic groups. The challenges they face may be compounded if their individual differences are not appreciated. In fact, an asset-oriented approach is essential to successful learning for students with disabilities. Like all students, they want to fit in and feel included as part of the class. No modifications, accommodations, or expert lesson plans can mitigate the feeling of not being accepted. Getting-to-know-you activities for all students are very important.

2. Utilize the Individual Education Program (IEP) or 504 Plan.

All students eligible for special education services are required to have an IEP, according to federal law. It is important to view the IEP as a working document. The IEP is developed by a multidisciplinary team in which "parents are considered equal partners with school personnel," according to the Individual with Disabilities Education Information Act, (IDEIA, 2004). In addition to demographic information, including the category of program eligibility and signature page, it is critical for teachers to be very familiar with the following IEP components and utilize them in instructional planning:

- student's current level of educational performance and social-emotional functioning;
- measurable goals and objectives to address individual needs;
- related services and program modification/supports;
- the extent to which the student will not participate in general education;
- the level of participation in district/state assessments and testing modification and accommodations, if any;
- transition services at age 16 (14 in California).

Of particular use in instructional planning are the IEP sections on current levels, goals and objectives, and modifications and supports.

3. Build collaboration between the general education and special education teachers.

It is required that students with disabilities be educated in the least restrictive environment. While that environment varies depending on the individual needs of the student, most students with mild and moderate disabilities are included in general education classrooms for much of the day with support from the special education teacher. Effective collaboration between the general education teacher and the special education teacher is essential. The general education teacher is often viewed as the grade-level curriculum expert while the special education teacher often provides resources and suggests modifications and accommodations. This collaboration should include co-designing instruction, joint progress monitoring, shared assessments, and co-teaching. For collaboration to be effective, it is very important that time be specifically given for this process.

Access and Equity

4. See *Accommodating Students with Special Needs Throughout the Literacy Block* to learn more about how to differentiate instruction using the specially designed features in *Benchmark Advance*.

This literacy program includes flexible grouping and differentiation for all students as well as repeated opportunities to individualize for a heterogeneous student population, including students with disabilities in English and Spanish. Numerous evidence-based instructional strategies that are effective for all learners are repeated throughout the Teacher Resource Systems. This section highlights features of the instruction that provide opportunities to differentiate content, process, and assessment. With this type of instructional materials, accommodations and modifications are a natural match. Teachers will find these carefully constructed differentiation strategies very helpful when planning and implementing literacy or biliteracy instruction.

There is no such thing as a one-size-fits-all accommodation or modification. You will want to strategically select the accommodation or modification that fits your individual student, maximizes on his/her strengths, and minimizes the impact of the disability.

As noted in the California Framework, "*accommodations* are changes that help a student to overcome or work around the disability. Accommodations do not reduce the learning or performance expectations but allow the student to complete an assignment or assessment with a change in presentation, response, setting, timing, or scheduling so that learners are provided equitable access during instruction and assessment.

"Unlike accommodations, *modifications* are adjustments to an assignment or assessment that changes what is expected or measured. Modifications should be used with caution as they alter, change, lower, or reduce learning expectations and can increase the gap between the achievement of students with disabilities and expectations for proficiency. Examples of modifications include the following:

• Reducing the expectations of an assignment or assessment (completing fewer problems, amount of materials, or level of problems to complete);

• Making assignments or assessment items easier;

• Providing clues to correct responses;

• Strategic use of primary language.

Accommodations and modifications should be designed on an individual student basis, not on the basis of category of disability.

When a student is taught by multiple teachers, it is recommended that accommodations and modifications be the same across instruction classroom tests. However, some accommodations and modifications may be appropriate only for instructional use and may not be appropriate for standardized assessments. It is very important that teachers are well informed about state policies regarding accommodations for state assessments.

What do I need to do differently for English learners with special needs?

Individual Education Programs for English learners with disabilities should include linguistically appropriate goals and objectives in addition to all the supports and services the student may require due to his or her disability. Typically, sheltering strategies are very powerful accommodations for students with special needs who are also English

©2018 Benchmark Education Company, LLC

Additional Resources **AR35**

Access and Equity

> **Recommended Resource:**
> **National Professional Development Center on Autism Spectrum Disorders**
> (http://autismpdc.fpg.unc.edu/content/briefs)

learners. Choose the strategies that meet both the learning need due to the disability and the current stage of English language development. Remember to think about the many aspects of the individual (culture, age, home language, socioeconomic level, and more). For example, wait time is both a common accommodation for students with disabilities who need additional time to process information and for English learners who require additional time to process the second language. Some of the strategies include visuals (photos, diagrams with labels, illustrations), manipulatives, realia (real objects), hands-on activities, total physical response (TPR), gestures, graphic organizers, sentence frames, and other accommodations that minimize language barriers and maximize comprehension of the concepts. It is important to note that under the Individuals with Disabilities Education Improvement Act (IDEIA), a student who is performing below grade level may not be determined to have a specific learning disability if the student's performance is primarily a result of limited English proficiency or is due to a lack of appropriate instruction.

What types of support are needed for students with Autism Spectrum Disorders?

As noted in Chapter 9 of the California ELA/ELD Framework, students with Autism Spectrum Disorders (ASD) represent the fastest growing population of students with disabilities. Students with ASD experience many challenges, especially in the area of social awareness—understanding how their behavior and actions affect others and interpreting the nonverbal cues (body language) of others (Constable, Grossi, Moniz, and Ryan 2013). Having difficulty recognizing and understanding the thoughts, feelings, beliefs, and intentions of others can be problematic in terms of achieving the Common Core English Language Arts standards that require communication and collaboration as well as those that require interpreting the feelings, thoughts, and intentions of characters or real persons. Teachers of students with ASD need to understand how these difficulties manifest themselves in the classroom in relation to the standards as well as how to provide instruction for these students to comprehend and write narratives related to the task at hand. Although some students with ASD are able to answer questions such as who, what, and where, they often struggle answering questions asking how and why. These issues become progressively more challenging as the demands to integrate information for various purposes increase at the secondary level. Teachers can find supports to enhance comprehension and ameliorate potentially anxious and stressful experiences by incorporating cognitive behavioral strategies identified by the National Professional Development Center on Autism Spectrum Disorders. Among important considerations are the following:

• Physically positioning oneself for face-to-face interactions and establishing attention;

• Providing verbal models for specific tasks;

• Responding to students' verbal and nonverbal initiations;

• Providing meaningful verbal feedback;

• Expanding students' utterances;

• Ensuring students have the prerequisite skills for a task;

• Breaking down tasks into manageable components;

• Knowing and using what students find motivating;

• Ensuring the use of appropriately challenging and interesting tasks.

Access and Equity

Meeting the Needs of Students Who Are Advanced Learners

By Marjorie McCabe, Ph.D. and Erin Marie Mason

> **Advanced Learners**
> Students who perform or have the potential to perform significantly above their age group. They may be formally identified as gifted and talented or not but demonstrate the capacity.

How can I recognize a range of advanced learners in my class?

In this section, we are focusing on students who perform or demonstrate the capacity to perform significantly above age-level peers in English Language Arts and English Language Development. Although it is up to each district to establish their own criteria for formal identification of advanced or gifted and talented learners, it is important for teachers to learn to recognize a range of advanced learners in their class and differentiate instruction to meet their needs whether formal identification exists or not. These students comprise a highly heterogeneous population, in terms of culture, language, ethnicity, socioeconomic level, gender, sexual orientation, age, and neurodiversity. It is especially common for advanced learners to go unrecognized when students exhibit their advanced learning in unfamiliar or inconsistent ways. In addition to the more familiar image of the "A" student who regularly masters grade-level concepts significantly faster than age-level peers, there is a much broader variety of advanced learners whose gifts and talents may go unnoticed on traditional measures of performance.

Tips for recognizing a range of advanced learners:

- Advanced learners do not necessarily demonstrate advanced performance uniformly across all areas. Advanced learning may present itself in spikes of achievement in the areas of talent or interest.

- Consider the stage of English language development for English learners, as well as their rate of progress. For example, imagine an English learner who begins the year with emerging English proficiency and is translating for peers by the end of the school year. This student may not demonstrate advanced abilities on typical English Language Arts tests yet. However, he or she may be best served by strategies for advanced learners since the student is exhibiting accelerated learning and talent in second language acquisition (or English language development).

- English learners will need sheltered instruction techniques to access the content and demonstrate their learning. Non-sheltered instructional strategies and assessments may not provide true opportunity to learn and may not reveal their advancement or talents.

- Students with disabilities can be twice exceptional. A student may have a disability that affects one area and may be gifted and talented in another.

- Students with behavioral challenges may exhibit significantly accelerated learning but may do so intermittently depending on the impact of the challenging behavior.

These identifications are not mutually exclusive, and in California's culturally and linguistically diverse population, many students will share identification in a variety of categories. In many ways, teachers can look for students who not only exhibit achievement or the capacity to achieve significantly above age-level peers, but in relation to their demographic peers. For example, is an English learner performing significantly beyond other English learners of their age who entered school at the same stage of English language development?

©2018 Benchmark Education Company, LLC

Additional Resources **AR37**

Access and Equity

Recommended Resources:

California Association for the Gifted
http://www.cagifted.org

National Association for Gifted Children
http://www.nagc.org

Educator 2 Educator - Curriculum & Materials
http://www.ed2ed.com

As the California ELA/ELD Framework outlines:

"A synthesis of research (Rogers 2007) on the education of students identified as gifted and talented suggests that they should be provided the following:

• Daily challenge in their specific areas of talent

• Regular opportunities to be unique and to work independently in their areas of passion and talent

• Various forms of subject-based and grade-based acceleration as their educational needs require

• Opportunities to socialize and learn with peers with similar abilities

• Instruction that is differentiated in pace, amount of review and practice, and organization of content presentation

Instruction for advanced learners should focus on depth and complexity. Opportunities to engage with appropriately challenging text and content, conduct research, use technology creatively, and write regularly on topics that interest them can be especially valuable for advanced learners; these experiences allow students to engage more deeply with content and may contribute to motivation. Instruction that focuses on depth and complexity ensures cohesion in learning rather than piecemeal "enrichment."

California Framework, Chapter 9: Access and Equity

How can I differentiate instruction to meet the needs of advanced learners?

All students can benefit from the types of strategies that support advanced learners. However, too often, advanced learners stagnate in their learning trajectory because the content, pace, and instructional processes do not meet their needs. This can lead to behavior issues, loss of interest in school, and a sense of not belonging with peers.

Assessment is key to determining content, pace and instructional processes. Pre-assessments and ongoing evaluation may be conducted formally or informally. Teacher observation is a powerful tool in detecting evidence of advanced learning, since it may not always be reflected on traditional assessments. Progress monitoring is essential to keeping instruction in the student's zone of proximal development. Students who demonstrate advanced learning or the potential for advanced learning may require:

• compacted content (advancing to more complex skills/concepts within the grade level or standards from future grade levels);

• accelerated pace of instruction (introduction of grade-level concepts, but with less time spent on each concept, practice, or review);

• variety of instructional processes (novelty of process or product, enhanced creativity, opportunities to apply standards to student's individual interests);

• opportunities to demonstrate biliteracy abilities in creative ways (for example, contrastive analysis of thematically related poetry/literature/lyrics in two languages, role play situational biliteracy contexts in academic content areas such as explaining the parts of cells and their functions in two languages).

Because *Benchmark Advance* is built around differentiated opportunities for student learning, it is an ideal instructional resource to support your students who are advanced learners. For example:

• A variety of formal and informal assessments allow teachers to pinpoint a student's zone of proximal development in two languages.

• Flexible grouping and small-group instruction for most reading and writing activities allows teachers to group student with similar levels of advancement or similar talents/interests.

• Flexible pacing and If/Then "Reinforce or Reaffirm the Strategy" instruction within the mini-lessons allow teachers to compact the content and accelerate the instruction in each lesson, within each standard, as needed.

• Leveled readers and trade book recommendations on each unit topic or concept allow teachers to customize reading instruction.

• E-books allow extensive variety of texts on topics that add depth and complexity, as well as novelty and variety.

• Research and writing opportunities engage students in creatively pursuing their unique interests and passions.

• Collaborative conversations allow students to customize learning to their interests and level of advancement.

Access and Equity

- A gradual release model (modeled, shared, guided, and independent activities) for speaking, listening, reading, and writing allows teachers to support a student's current stage of development while preparing them to master the next stage. Teachers can move students along a continuum of depth and complexity as needed.

- Project-based learning "Connect Across Disciplines" learning opportunities to promote innovation and social responsibility.

Accommodating Students with Special Needs Throughout the *Benchmark Advance* Literacy Block

As you get to know your individual students with disabilities and their current levels of performance, pay attention to the areas in which they struggle. If their disability manifests itself in one area, provide an alternate pathway for them to access the standards, while supporting growth as much as possible in the area of challenge. The chart on the following pages points out many of the opportunities for differentiated instruction already integrated into the *Benchmark Advance* literacy block, and it suggests some additional accommodations that can implemented within your whole- and small-group instruction. These accommodations will help you meet the needs of students with a range of disabilities as well as the needs of advanced learners.

Struggling readers will benefit by direct, explicit code instruction in phonemic awareness and word identification strategies as part of a balanced literacy instruction program. Also, the use of implicit instruction, which focuses on context clues and picture cues, will be valuable. The use of systematic phonemic awareness and phonics instruction and numerous opportunities for practice and review will be key to successful learning by students with disabilities.

It is essential to get to know your students as individuals. If they are students with disabilities, it is crucial to review the IEP or 504 Plan and build collaboration between the general education and special education teachers serving the student. The same strategy could soothe one student yet aggravate another, empower one child yet incapacitate another, depending on how the disability manifests itself. For example, a student with sensory processing issues may shut down with a sandpaper phonics activity, while a student without such sensitivities may require that stimulus and thrive with it. Your broader knowledge of the student, your detailed progress monitoring, and your collaboration will allow you to distinguish which strategies are the best fit for the student.

Benchmark Advance also includes intervention materials for efficient and effective use in tutorial or small-group instructional settings. These materials focus on students who need re-teaching and practice in one or more of the four identified key foundational skills in English and/or in Spanish that are part of the Reading Standards: Foundational Skills in the CA CCSS for ELA: (1) print concepts; (2) phonological awareness; (3) phonics and word recognition; and (4) fluency.

Many of the strategies included in the following chart were adapted from those recommended in *Strategies for Teaching Students with Learning and Behavior Problems* [Vaughn, S. & Bos, C. (2012). Boston, MA: Pearson].

©2018 Benchmark Education Company, LLC

Additional Resources **AR39**

Access and Equity

Accommodating Students with Special Needs Throughout the Literacy Block—Grades K–2

Grades K–2 Literacy Block Component	Lesson activities to support through accommodations	Disabilities that affect oral language (speaking and listening)	Disabilities that affect decoding	
Interactive Read-Aloud	Listening to complex read-alouds	- Ask frequent questions to check for comprehension. - Provide visual cues such as photos, illustrations, gestures, and facial expressions. - Pause throughout the text to allow students to make connections and note their ideas in a journal.	n/a	
	Summarizing and responding to read-alouds	- Have students express ideas by developing drawings or selecting from pre-made photos and visuals. - Students may benefit from preparing and formulating a response with a partner. - Provide sentence frames. - Use technology, such as typing a response and sending it to the teacher or posting on an electronic chart realtime such as a wiki or discussion forum.	n/a	
Shared Reading	Developing concepts about print	- Use a pointer to model one-to-one correspondence between the actual features of the real book and the discussion.	n/a	
	Reading aloud to build fluency	- Scaffolding is built into the mini-lessons through picture walk, choral reading, and gradual release of teacher modeling (I do, we do). Students join choral reading as they are ready. - Repeated readings build confidence, familiarity, and fluency. - Add gestures, facial expressions, and total physical response to enhance comprehension.	- Scaffolding is built into the mini-lessons through picture walk, choral reading, and gradual release of teacher modeling. - Use a pointer to model one-to-one correspondence between oral and written words.	
	Developing language knowledge	- Use graphic organizers and charts that illustrate word patterns and features. - Highlight key words and word features written in the text using a frame in the big book or by using the highlighting or window shade features in the e-presenter version of the text.	- Provide opportunities to hear and discuss word patterns and features in cooperative groups or pairs.	
Reading/ Shared Writing Mini-Lessons	Participating in Collaborative Conversations	- Use the Observation Checklist for Collaborative Conversation (found in each week of instruction) to help you identify communication skills to model for your students. - Provide sentence frames to support the kind of conversation you expect. (You may wish to download copies of the Think-Speak-Listen Flip Book, which contains frames to support academic conversations.) - Allow students to write or draw to express their ideas during discussions. - Make laptops or tablets available for students to keyboard their responses to conversation prompts.	n/a	
	Participating in Productive Engagement Activities	- Use the Observation Checklist for Productive Engagement (found in Weeks 2 and 3) to help you monitor students during learning tasks and make minute-by-minute instructional decisions based on their needs. - Based on your observations, adjust the content and pace of instruction. - Provide additional gradual release instruction using the model/guided practice or If/Then strategies.	- Use the Observation Checklist for Productive Engagement (found in Weeks 2 and 3) to help you monitor students during learning tasks and make minute-by-minute instructional decisions based on their needs. - Based on your observations, adjust the content and pace of instruction. - Provide additional gradual release instruction using the model/guided practice or If/Then strategies.	

AR40 Additional Resources

©2018 Benchmark Education Company, LLC

Access and Equity

Disabilities that affect reading comprehension	Disabilities that affect written expression	Accommodations for advanced learners
n/a	n/a	- Pause to allow students to make connections and note their ideas in a journal. - Adjust the pace to allow students to spend more time on a particular section that inspires them or to listen to longer segments and then analyze the whole.
- Provide pictures or visuals to aide with sequencing, main ideas and details, and retelling.	- Have students express ideas by developing drawings or selecting from pre-made photos and visuals. - Students may benefit from processing and formulating a response with a partner. - Provide sentence frames to support student responses. You may wish to download copies of the Think-Speak-Listen Flip Book	- Group students with like interests or similar accelerated learning needs in a think-pair-share or team discussion. - Ask students to compare the text with other complex texts, with other authors, or with texts on the same topic from other content areas, in order to identify patterns. - Invite students to consider multiple perspectives, such as the point of view of different characters or professionals from different disciplines related to the text.
n/a	n/a	- Formally or informally pre-assess to identify who has mastered these concepts at the start of instruction. (Screeners may be found in the K–2 Reading Foundational Skills Assessment Handbook.) - Teach a mini-lesson on more advanced concepts of print to those who need it. - Group students who have mastered these concepts and have them create their own book that includes key concepts of print that they have already mastered.
- Scaffolding is built into the mini-lessons through picture walk, choral reading, and gradual release of teacher modeling. - Add gestures, facial expressions, and total physical response (TPR) to enhance comprehension.	n/a	- Allow the students who decode fluently after the picture walk or first read to create gestures or actions to accompany the read-aloud. - Ask students who are decoding at an advanced level to focus on expressive reading, prosody (e.g., intonation, voice, and phrasing to convey their understanding of characters and mood).
- Use visual aids (photos, sketches, icons) to support comprehension of the key words being studied. - Use gestures and total physical response to support comprehension of the key words. - Use graphic organizers and charts that illustrate word patterns and features. - Highlight key words and word features written in the text.	- Students can express their ideas through verbal discussions or visual representations (diagrams or charts). - Use sentence frames to scaffold written expression. - Use graphic organizers to list key phrases, rather than full sentences or paragraphs in some cases. - Utilize assistive technology (writing on a computer, dictating to computer).	- Adjust the type of language students study in the lesson to meet their zone of proximal development. Provide more advanced content (language) or accelerate the pace and move to independent practice or application more quickly. - Strategically pair students for discussion with other students who share their passions or accelerated learning needs. - Ask students to think like a linguist or an author and identify new words that fit the pattern. They may use a graphic organizer or chart to expand on the lesson's ideas. - For advanced learners who are also English learners, ask them to apply the lesson to their primary language and chart examples from that language. Compare and contrast how the pattern in English is similar or different from the pattern in the primary language.
n/a	- Allow students to express their ideas in pictures or through role playing. - Provide a sentence frame for students to use. - Consider timekeeper, reporter, or discussion director as strategic roles.	- Provide opportunities for students to make connections across texts, authors, and genre. - Challenge students to pose new questions and to identify connections between the text and their other content area studies. - Provide more challenging group roles and responsibilities. - Use the Challenge Activities provided in many of the Weeks 2 and 3 Close Reading mini-lessons.
- Use the Observation Checklist for Productive Engagement (found in Weeks 2 and 3) to help you monitor students during learning tasks and make minute-by-minute instructional decisions based on their needs. - Based on your observations, adjust the content and pace of instruction. - Provide additional gradual release instruction using the model/guided practice or If/Then strategies.	- Use the Observation Checklist for Productive Engagement (found in Weeks 2 and 3) to help you monitor students during learning tasks and make minute-by-minute instructional decisions based on their needs. - Based on your observations, adjust the content and pace of instruction. - Provide additional gradual release instruction using the model/guided practice or If/Then strategies.	- Use the Observation Checklist for Productive Engagement (found in Weeks 2 and 3) to help you monitor students during learning tasks and make minute-by-minute instructional decisions based on their needs. - Accelerate the content based on progress monitoring. Move to above-grade-level content where/when indicated by formal and informal assessment. - Students may need all concepts taught but for a shorter time, with less repetition and at an accelerated pace. - Use progress monitoring to form a temporary, flexible group of students who are ready for advancement in a particular standard.

©2018 Benchmark Education Company, LLC

Access and Equity

Accommodating Students with Special Needs Throughout the Literacy Block—Grades K–2

Grades K–2 Literacy Block Component	Lesson activities to support through accommodations	Disabilities that affect oral language (speaking and listening)	Disabilities that affect decoding	
Reading/Shared Writing Mini-Lessons	Text Annotation (Grade 2)	n/a	- Model text annotation skills as needed. Refer to the annotation symbols on the inside front cover of each unit's Texts for Close Reading. - Consider using a leveled reader that addresses the same content and concepts, but at the student's current reading level. Allow the student to annotate this leveled reader using self-stick notes or the notetaking feature in the e-reader version on BenchmarkUniverse.com. - Allow partner or buddy reading and discussion while creating annotated notes.	
	Writing	n/a	- During the revising and editing process when decoding is most required, allow students to work in pairs. - Allow the use of electronic spelling and grammar checks to help students identify text that needs correction. - Use assistive technology so the device reads the written text back to the student for review.	
Phonics	Phonemic Awareness	- Use the Pre-Teach/Re-Teach Phonemic Awareness Routine to provide additional practice with phonemic awareness skills. - Use counters with the Elkonin boxes on the student work mats to visually and kinesthetically help students build awareness of the number and order of sounds they hear. - Try clapping or gesturing to count or mark sounds.	n/a	
	Letter/Sound Correspondence	- Use the Pre-Teach/Re-Teach Letter/Sound Correspondences Routine to provide additional instruction and practice. - Reinforce letter/sound correspondences using the Frieze Cards and other visuals. - Use letter tiles that can be manipulated and moved as students say each sound. - Provide longer and more frequent opportunities for modeled, guided, and independent practice. - Conduct more frequent progress monitoring to check for understanding and mastery.	- Use the Pre-Teach/Re-Teach Letter/Sound Correspondences Routine to provide additional instruction and practice. - Reinforce letter/sound correspondences using the Frieze Cards and other visuals. - Use letter tiles that can be manipulated and moved as students say each sound. - Provide longer and more frequent opportunities for modeled, guided, and independent practice. - Conduct more frequent progress monitoring to check for understanding and mastery.	
	Blending	- Use the Pre-Teach/Re-Teach Blending Routine to provide additional instruction and practice. - As you model blends, elongate the sounds as you pronounce them. - Use letter tiles that can be manipulated and moved as students say the sounds. - Provide longer and more frequent opportunities for modeled, guided, and independent practice. - Conduct more frequent progress monitoring to check for understanding and mastery.	- Use the Pre-Teach/Re-Teach Blending Routine to provide additional instruction and practice. - As you model blends, elongate the sounds as you pronounce them. - Use letter tiles that can be manipulated and moved as students say the sounds. - Provide longer and more frequent opportunities for modeled, guided, and independent practice. - Conduct more frequent progress monitoring to check for understanding and mastery.	

AR42 Additional Resources

©2018 Benchmark Education Company, LLC

Access and Equity

Disabilities that affect reading comprehension	Disabilities that affect written expression	Accommodations for advanced learners
- Model text annotation skills as needed. Refer to the annotation symbols on the inside front cover of each unit's Texts for Close Reading. - Teach students to note words that are not familiar. - Students may use the e-reader version of the text to highlight words or phrases they wish to clarify or practice, paraphrase them, or write notes.	- Students may highlight, underline, or circle key parts of text using the consumable or the e-reader version. - Annotated notes may be taken electronically in the e-reader version of the text. - Notes may take the form of diagrams, visuals, charts, or key phrases.	- Add complexity by allowing students to use text annotation to compare text elements or information with other texts or authors or across content areas. - Add complexity by asking students to analyze the text/information from the perspective of different characters or professions (disciplines), such as a historian, an economist, an ecologist, a lawyer, etc. - Add depth by asking students to note additional information based on their interests, cite other sources they have read, and compare/contrast information or opinions. - Add depth by asking students to cite key evidence in support of a particular overarching theme such as ethics, change, systems, etc. - (See Sandra Kaplan's *Icons of Depth and Complexity.*)
- n/a	- Allow the full writing process to take place using a computer or tablet. Avoid having students write or rewrite drafts by hand. - Pre-writes may be illustrated or use graphic organizers with key phrases. - Provide sentence frames specific to the genre or text structure. Practice them orally prior to using them in writing. - Provide models of the desired type of writing, anchor papers, and rubrics with examples. (See the exemplars provided in the mini-lessons and Informal Assessment Handbook.) - Use illustrated graphic organizers to explain the key elements of the text/genre, such as a checklist with a visual or icon to represent each item. - Allow students to work in pairs or teams. - Allow the use of spelling and grammar checks to help student's identify text that needs correction. - Use assistive technology so the device reads the written text back to the student for review.	- Allow the full writing process to take place using a computer or tablet. Avoid having students write or rewrite drafts by hand if it reduces their pace of thinking/production. - Support more sophisticated, advanced language through sentence frames. - Provide models of more advanced writing, anchor papers, and rubrics with examples from the current grade or the next grade level (See the Informal Assessment Handbook). - Allow students to work in pairs or teams by interest/passion or zone of proximal development. - Allow the use of spelling and grammar checks to help students identify text that needs correction and maintain the pace of their creative process and thought process. - Use assistive technology so the device reads the written text back to the student for review. - For students who are advanced learners and English learners, allow them to write any part of the pre-write or rough draft in the primary language to support the pace and sophistication of thinking/writing.
n/a	n/a	- Use progress monitoring to continually provide activities in students' zone of proximal development. Accelerate the pace of instruction as needed. Once automaticity is acquired, move on. - Provide more complex words and sound combinations.
n/a	- Try multimodality approaches such as writing the letter in sand or in shaving cream, tracing the letter with a finger on sandpaper or textured surface, placing moveable letters on the work mat or a magnetic board. - Use technology to allow students to select printed letters, manipulate them, and draw them on a screen. - Use assistive technology to dictate letters to the computer or tablet.	- Use progress monitoring to continually provide activities in students' zone of proximal development. Accelerate the pace of instruction as needed. Once automaticity is acquired, move on. - If students are decoding and comprehending text independently, proceed to small group and independent reading activities. - Provide more complex words and sound combinations.
n/a	- Try multimodality approaches such as writing the letter in sand or in shaving cream, tracing the letter with a finger on sandpaper or textured surface, placing moveable letters on a magnetic board. - Use technology to allow students to select printed letters, manipulate them, or draw them on a screen. - Use assistive technology to dictate letters to the computer or tablet.	- Use progress monitoring to continually provide activities in students' zone of proximal development. Accelerate the pace of instruction as needed. Once automaticity is acquired, move on. - Provide more complex words and sound combinations. - If students are decoding and comprehending text independently, proceed to small group and independent reading activities.

©2018 Benchmark Education Company, LLC

Access and Equity

Accommodating Students with Special Needs Throughout the Literacy Block—Grades K–2

Grades K–2 Literacy Block Component	Lesson activities to support through accommodations	Disabilities that affect oral language (speaking and listening)	Disabilities that affect decoding	
Phonics	High-Frequency Word Instruction	- Use the Pre-Teach/Re-Teach High-Frequency Words Routine to provide additional instruction and practice. - Teach the most frequently occurring words. - Use words in meaningful contexts and make sure students understand word meaning. - Limit the number of words introduced in a single lesson. - Utilize multimodality systems, such as tracing, copying and writing from memory. - Provide multiple opportunities to practice words by building, reading, and writing words until automaticity occurs.	n/a	
	Spelling			
	Handwriting	If students have difficulty recognizing sounds they hear, it will affect their ability to write them.	n/a	

AR44 Additional Resources

©2018 Benchmark Education Company, LLC

Access and Equity

Disabilities that affect reading comprehension	Disabilities that affect written expression	Accommodations for advanced learners
- Use the Pre-Teach/Re-Teach High-Frequency Words Routine to provide additional instruction and practice. - Teach the most frequently occurring words. - Use words in meaningful contexts and make sure students understand word meaning. - Limit the number of words introduced in a single lesson. - Utilize multimodality systems, such as tracing, copying, and writing from memory. - Provide multiple opportunities to practice words by building, reading, and writing words until automaticity occurs.	- Try multimodality approaches such as writing the high-frequency word in sand or in shaving cream, tracing the letters with a finger on sandpaper or textured surface, or placing moveable letters on a magnetic board. - Use technology to allow students to select printed letters, manipulate them, or draw them on a screen. - Use assistive technology to dictate letters to the computer or tablet.	- Use progress monitoring to continually provide activities in students' zone of proximal development. - If students are decoding and comprehending text independently, proceed to small-group and independent reading activities. - Provide more complex words and sound combinations.
	- Analyze current level of functioning in students' written work and dictation by determining the type and pattern of errors. - Develop spelling instructional program based on individual needs as evidenced in assessment. - Look for error patterns. - Make sure students can read and understand the meaning of each spelling word. - Reduce the number of words introduced—no more than three words at a time - Spelling is taught concurrently with phonics in the program so that students see a connection between reading and spelling. Reinforce this as much as possible to scaffold them. - Teach words with same spelling patterns and include non-examples. - Give many opportunities to practice spelling complete words correctly using a model and self-checking for mastery. - Use the Re-teach/Pre-teach Spelling Routine to provide additional modeling and guided practice. - Provide frequent opportunities for seeing and using mastered words in context. - Review mastered words while introducing new words. - Avoid having students simply write the words over and over from memory without checking a model and getting feedback. - Use high-frequency words so students can see same words in reading texts. - Use a combination of approaches, such as multi-sensory, technology supports. - Have students say the words while writing it or spelling it aloud with a partner. - Have students write a spelling word while teacher or partner simultaneously displays the correct model. Then delay the amount of time before the correct model is shown until students write the word from memory. - Students compare their incorrectly spelled words with correct model.	- Use progress monitoring to continually provide activities in their zone of proximal development. - Provide more complex spelling words and sound combinations.
n/a	Have students write with a keyboard or a touch screen if they have sensory issues with the physical handwriting process.	- n/a

©2018 Benchmark Education Company, LLC

Additional Resources **AR45**

Access and Equity

Accommodating Students with Special Needs Throughout the Literacy Block—Grades K–2

Grades K–2 Literacy Block Component	Lesson activities to support through accommodations	Disabilities that affect oral language (speaking and listening)	Disabilities that affect decoding	
Small Group Reading/ Independent & Collaborative Activities	Reading leveled texts	- Small-group reading may be conducted with fewer students. - Use buddy reading to alternate reading and listening activities, shorten the length of listening/decoding segments, and allow students to focus on comprehension.	- Precede a difficult book with an easier book on the same topic that uses similar language. - Reading books in a series is a tremendous support (same topic or characters). - Small reading groups may be conducted with fewer students. - Use partner reading to alternate reading and listening activities, shorten the length of listening/decoding segments, and allow students to focus on comprehension. - Allow more frequent and repeated readings of text. - Have students record themselves reading on a laptop or tablet, measure words per minute, and hear their intonation and prosody.	
	Reading reader's theater scripts	- Have students record themselves reading on a laptop or tablet, measure words per minute, and hear their intonation and prosody.	- Remind students to use the color-coding in their scripts to help them find and track their parts. - Have students record themselves reading on a laptop or tablet, measure words per minute, and hear their intonation and prosody. - Invite students to read along with the audio-highlighted e-reader version of the script.	
	Performing reader's theater scripts	- Explicitly teach presentation or public speaking skills including volume, intonation, eye contact, body positioning, facial expressions, and more. - Allow students to read aloud only when fully confident or give them small groups in which they perform. - Allow students to create an audio or video recording to capture the performance in which they are the most successful.	- Assign parts or roles to students based on their reading level. Match the role to the student's reading level using the Characters/Levels chart for each script (in the Reader's Theater Teacher Handbook). - Pair students to allow buddy reading as a pre-reading support before reading publicly to a larger group.	

AR46 Additional Resources

©2018 Benchmark Education Company, LLC

Access and Equity

Disabilities that affect reading comprehension	Disabilities that affect written expression	Accommodations for advanced learners
- Precede a difficult book with an easier book on the same topic that uses similar language. - Reading books in a series is a tremendous support (same characters or topic). - Use text-specific graphic organizers, story maps, or illustrations to chart key points for comprehension. - Provide visuals, such as diagrams, drawings, and photos from the text to support the student in discussing the text (sequence/retell/summarize). - Use buddy reading to alternate reading and listening activities, shorten the length of listening/decoding segments, and allow students to focus on comprehension.	n/a	- If students are decoding and comprehending text independently, provide texts at advanced levels, including above grade level. The small-group texts for each unit include titles at a range of guided reading levels. See also the list of trade book recommendations provided for each grade level. - Allow the students who decode fluently after the first read to create gestures or actions to accompany the read-aloud. - Ask students who are decoding at an advanced level to focus on expressive reading, prosody (e.g. intonation, voice, and phrasing to convey their understanding of characters and mood). - Students with similar interests and reading levels may form literature circles and research teams.
- Use the gradual release modeling and practice in the Reader's Theater Teacher Handbook lessons to support comprehension through read-aloud, shared reading, and discussion of the characters, plot, and key ideas or themes. - Use the explicit vocabulary instruction to support comprehension. - Extend think aloud to model metacognition to students. For example, provide repeated modeling on how to make connections between events and ideas in the text. - Explicitly teach students self-monitoring strategies for identifying words or language that is confusing or unknown. Then provide extended guided practice in applying the strategies. - Use graphic organizers to visually and explicitly teach connections between ideas in the text (cause and effect, inferences, author's intent, main idea, etc.).	n/a	- Have advanced learners read and rehearse the more challenging script provided for each unit. - Consult Characters/Levels chart for each script and assign advanced readers higher level roles or roles that require a more nuanced, expressive interpretation. - Allow more passionate, interested advanced readers to be understudies for other parts/roles. - Individuals or a group can create a text extension, an alternate plot twist, or interaction between texts.
- Acting out and role-playing scenes can provide total physical response and kinesthetic approach to enhance comprehension. - Chunk scenes into smaller segments to explain passages, phrases, or inferences that are challenging.	n/a	- Allow students to use technology to present reader's theater via podcast/audio presentation, video, puppet show. - Create an improvisational theater experience, based on the original script that asks students to create their own language/text in the style of the original with new events, ideas, and actions.

©2018 Benchmark Education Company, LLC

Contrastive Analysis of English and Nine World Languages

The Value of Contrastive Analysis

By Silvia Dorta-Duque de Reyes and Jill Kerper-Mora, Ph.D.

Benchmark Advance Contrastive Analysis Charts

The Sound-Spelling Contrastive Analysis Charts compare the phonemes (sounds) and graphemes (letters) of English to nine world languages and enable teachers to compare various features at a glance, including:

• Categories of English spellings (grapheme types, such as short vowels)

• English sounds (phonemes)

• English letter(s) (the most common grapheme(s) used to represent the sound)

• Examples of English sounds in various positions in words (initial, medial, and final position)

• Whether that sound exists in each of the nine languages

• Whether the letter(s) that represent that sound exist in each language

Contrastive analysis is the systematic study of two languages to identify their similarities and differences. Contrastive analysis charts help educators recognize distinctions between a student's primary language and English. The Benchmark Advance Contrastive Analysis Charts address the similarities and differences between English and nine of the most common world languages spoken by English learners in California.

For both students and teachers, using a language construction process that recognizes the similarities and differences between a primary and secondary language, rather than an error correction procedure, builds students' awareness of how English works. In every contrastive analysis lesson, students benefit when their primary language is respected and tapped as a resource for learning English through an additive approach that honors their primary language.

All oral languages are comprised of phonemes, and each of those sounds is articulated in a particular position in the mouth. As teachers are helping students to recognize and pronounce the sounds of English (phonology), they need to know whether the students' primary language utilizes particular sounds. If the target sound is found in the student's primary language, it will be fairly easy for the student to articulate and use that sound in English. If, however, the sound is not found in the student's primary language, teachers will need to provide additional instruction and support to ensure that students "hear" (discriminate) and articulate the sound in English.

Students will need instruction in recognizing and distinguishing the sounds of English as compared to or contrasted with sounds in their primary language (e.g., vowels, consonants, consonant blends, syllable structures). An example is the short vowel sounds of English that are not equivalent to vowel sounds in Spanish. In an alphabetic language system, phonology and phonemic awareness are the foundation for reading and writing.

There are many writing systems in the world. Latin-based languages, such as English and Spanish, use a writing system that is based on the letters of the alphabet; words are formed by combining different letters. Other languages, such as Chinese, use a completely different system of writing. It is called the logographic system. Each character represents a meaningful (morphological) unit. Because these two systems are entirely different, there is not a basis for comparison of the writing systems. For students who have been taught to use the logographic system, an introduction to the alphabet is necessary, and the instruction needs to include the sound–symbol relationship.

Contrastive Analysis of English and Nine World Languages

The Structure of the Sound-Spelling Contrastive Analysis Charts

In order to support students who are acquiring new sounds and letters in a new language, it is important to map out which sounds and letters are familiar to students, the extent to which the sounds and letters are familiar, and which sounds and letters are new and unfamiliar. The charts indicate whether the English phonemes and graphemes exist in both languages (positive), are about the same (approximate), or have no equivalency.

Transfer Indicators in the Charts	What They Mean
Yes	There is an equivalent, or positive, transfer relationship between English and student's primary language.
Approximate	This term is used when referring to phoneme variants that are considered close enough to the corresponding English language sound not to cause confusion for English learners.
No	There is no equivalent or transfer relationship between English and the student's primary language.

Although some world languages use an alphabetic system for writing (e.g., Spanish, Vietnamese), they each vary in both sounds and symbols used to encode those sounds. Some sounds and spellings are fully transferable (e.g., sound /b/ can be encoded with letter *b* in both Spanish and English, as in [botón/button]). Some sounds that are transferable can be encoded in English using spelling patterns *not* found in primary language (e.g., /k/ spelled *ck* in English, as in *duck*).

The Structure of the Grammar-Syntax Charts

The Grammar-Syntax charts are aligned to the CCSS Language standards and compare the grammatical differences between English and each of the nine world languages. The charts are divided into the conventions of standard English grammar: verbs; nouns; word order; adverbs and adjectives; pronouns; and prepositions, conjunctions, and articles.

These charts provide teachers with information relating to potential error patterns that may result as students generalize what they know and use in their home language to English. Once teachers know which grammatical structures transfer to academic English conventions, and which do not, they can adjust instruction to provide maximum reinforcement for skills lessons on these structures. For example, English is an inflectional language. In an inflectional language, verbs change forms. For example, the verb "see" can appear as "see," "sees," "saw," "seen," or "seeing." Other languages, such as Chinese, are non-inflectional. Words/verbs do not change shapes. The word "see" 看 is always written as 看 and there is no change. In addition, the word "to" in front of an English "verb" such as "to go" is nonexistent.

When teachers learn to identify and capitalize on students' existing language skills, they are able to use positive transfer to support student in gaining English language proficiency and biliteracy. Instructional approaches that promote students' awareness of and understandings about language variety are particularly useful for supporting students' metalinguistic knowledge and positive language identity.

We extend our appreciation to the language consultants, educators, and linguists who reviewed these charts for accuracy and completeness, and we extend special recognition to Sandra Ceja, who compiled these charts.

Using Contrastive Analysis to Inform Instruction

The Contrastive Analysis Charts give teachers information about students' native language usages, structures, and grammar to enable them to accomplish the following:

1. Support students' overall understanding of how English works in ways that are similar to or different from usages in their native language.

2. Identify specific teaching points where metalinguistic knowledge of linguistic similarities and differences will enable students to self-monitor and correct errors and error patterns in English in both oral and written production. This includes teachers' use of phonological differences between students' primary language and English that impact their pronunciation and spelling.

3. Scaffold and support students' developing strategies in gaining word level meaning of English forms, such as nominalization (converting a verb to a noun) and noting the way English words are formed (morphology), such as prefixes, root word, and suffixes that support students in deciphering new vocabulary based on their knowledge of their native language. This is especially helpful in learning cognates.

4. Scaffold and support students in developing language learning strategies for increasing their ability in sentence and clause-level meaning-making strategies of sentence deconstruction ("unpacking sentences") and for understanding phrase level meaning conveyed through English grammar and syntax in informational and literary text.

©2018 Benchmark Education Company, LLC

Additional Resources **AR49**

Contrastive Analysis of English and Nine World Languages

Sound-Spelling: Consonants

	Sound (phoneme)	English Most Common Spelling Patterns (graphemes)	English Notes	English Word Examples			Spanish Sound (phoneme) transfer?	Spanish Spelling pattern (grapheme) transfer?	Vietnamese Sound (phoneme) transfer?	Vietnamese Spelling pattern (grapheme) transfer?	Hmong Sound (phoneme) transfer?	Hmong Spelling pattern (grapheme) transfer?
Consonants				initial	medial	final						
The sound /b/ is used or approximated in all of these languages, but the spelling used to communicate /b/ varies.	/b/	b	Subject to medial consonant doubling. Consonant blends include bl and br. Spelling b(e) in long vowel syllables	button	cabin (bubble)	lab (cube)	yes	yes	yes	yes	approx.	no
The sound /k/ is used in all of these languages, but the spelling used to communicate /k/ varies.	/k/	c	Primarily followed by another consonant, or short/long a, o, u vowel sound. Consonant blends include cl and cr.	castle	act	music	yes	yes	yes	yes	yes	no
		k	Primarily followed by short/long e, i vowel sound	karate	monkey	mask		yes		yes		yes
		_ck	Following short vowel sound at the end of a syllable or word	(n/a)	blacksmith	duck		no		no		no
		-lk	Low frequency when preceded by o or a	(n/a)	chalky, yolks	talk, folk		no		no		no
		ch	Greek words	chorus,	echo	stomach, ache		no		no		no
		qu, que	French	quay	conquer	antique		yes (qu but not que)		no		no
The sound /d/ is used or approximated in most of these languages, but the spelling used to communicate /d/ varies.	/d/	d	Subject to medial consonant doubling. Consonant blends include dr and dw	dice	maiden (paddle)	mad (add)	approx.	yes	yes	yes	yes	yes
The sound /f/ is used or approximated in many of these languages, but the spelling used to communicate /f/ varies.	/f/	f	Subject to medial consonant doubling. Consonant blends include fr and fl.	family	after (baffle)	self, knife, muff	yes	yes	yes	no	yes	yes
		gh	-ough and -augh patterns	(n/a)	laughter	enough		no		no		no
		ph		photo	aphid	graph		no		yes		no
The sound /g/ is used or approximated in many of these languages, but the spelling used to communicate /g/ varies.	/g/	g	"Hard g" sound, mainly when followed by a, o, u. There are exceptions (girl, get and others). Subject to medial consonant doubling. Consonant blends include gr and gl. /gw/ sound spelled with gu (language, penguin)	goal	drags (baggage)	tag, (egg)	yes	yes	yes	yes	approx.	no
		gu ("silent u")	"Hard g" sound spelled gu when followed by e, l, or y to prevent "soft g" sound	guide	intrigued	(gue) league, plague		yes		no		
		gh		ghost	aghast			no		yes		no

AR50 Additional Resources

©2018 Benchmark Education Company, LLC

Contrastive Analysis of English and Nine World Languages

Sound (phoneme)	Most Common Spelling Patterns (graphemes)	Tagalog Sound (phoneme) transfer?	Tagalog Spelling pattern (grapheme) transfer?	Korean Sound (phoneme) transfer?	Korean Spelling pattern (grapheme) transfer?	Cantonese Sound (phoneme) transfer?	Cantonese Spelling pattern (grapheme) transfer?	Mandarin Sound (phoneme) transfer?	Mandarin Spelling pattern (grapheme) transfer?	Farsi Sound (phoneme) transfer?	Farsi Spelling pattern (grapheme) transfer?	Arabic Sound (phoneme) transfer?	Arabic Spelling pattern (grapheme) transfer?
/b/	b	yes	yes	approx.	no	approx.	no	no	no	yes		yes	
/k/	c	yes	no	yes	no	yes	no	yes	no	yes	no	yes	no
	k		yes		no		no		no		no		no
	_ck		no		no		no		no		no		no
	-lk		no		no		no		no		no		no
	ch		no		no		no		no		no		no
	qu, que		no		no		no		no		no		no
/d/	d	yes	no	approx.	no	approx.	no	no	no	yes	no	yes	no
/f/	f	no	no	no	no	yes	no	yes	no	yes	no	yes	no
	gh		no		no		no		no		no		no
	ph		no		no		no		no		no		no
/g/	g	yes	yes	approx.	no	approx.	no	no	no	yes	no	no	no
	gu ('silent u')		no					no	no		no		no
	gh		no		no		no	no	no		no		no

©2018 Benchmark Education Company, LLC

Contrastive Analysis of English and Nine World Languages

Sound-Spelling: Consonants

	English						Spanish		Vietnamese		Hmong	
	Sound (phoneme)	Most Common Spelling Patterns (graphemes)	Notes	Word Examples			Sound (phoneme) transfer?	Spelling pattern (grapheme) transfer?	Sound (phoneme) transfer?	Spelling pattern (grapheme) transfer?	Sound (phoneme) transfer?	Spelling pattern (grapheme) transfer?
The sound /h/ is used or approximated in many of these languages, but the spelling used to communicate /h/ varies.	/h/	h_	/h/ sound in English occurs only at the beginning of a syllable and never as the final sound in a word. When not in the first syllable, it is paired with a consonant ch, gh, rh, ph, sh, th, or wh.	hip	enhance		approx.	no	yes	yes	yes	yes
The sound /j/ is used or approximated in some of these languages, but the spelling used to communicate /j/ varies.	/j/	j	j used at the beginning of a syllable. ge or dge used for /j/ at the end of a word or syllable. Few exceptions (algae, margarine)	jam	inject		no	no	approx.	no	no	no
		ge	"Soft g" when followed by e. Final /j/ sound when part of a long vowel/final e pattern.	gems	angel	page		no		no		no
		gi_	"Soft g" when followed by i	gist	margin			no		no		no
		gy	"Soft g" when followed by y	gym	biology			no		no		no
		_dge	Used as /j/ spelling at the end of a syllable when following a short vowel sound		badger	wedge		no		no		no
		du	More complex Latin words		gradual, educate			no		no		no
		di	Lower frequency, more complex words		soldier			no		no		no
The sound /l/ is used or approximated in all of these languages, and the common spelling used to communicate /l/ is l among the alphabetic languages.	/l/	l	Used as spelling for initial sound of a syllable and the last sound of a consonant blend (bl, cl, chl, fl, gl, pl, sl, spl). Doubled when adding suffix -ly (equal --> equally).	lion	melt, (follow)	girl	yes	yes	yes	yes	yes	yes
		ll	More frequently used than l at the end of a syllable after short vowel	yellow	bell			no		no		no
		-el	English suffix			tunnel		no		no		no
		_le	English suffix, used more often than -el. When added to a closed syllable, can influence consonant doubling (i.e., ap-ple, bab-ble).			maple		no		no		no
The sound /m/ is used or approximated in all of these languages, and the common spelling used to communicate /m/ is m among the alphabetic languages.	/m/	m	Most common spelling, can be subject to medial consonant doubling (hammock).	medal	hamper	ham, become	yes	yes	yes	yes	yes	yes
		mn	Low frequency. When adding affixes, can "cause" both letters to be pronounced (i.e., autumn --> autumnal)		condemned	hymn		no		no		no

AR52 Additional Resources

©2018 Benchmark Education Company, LLC

Sound (phoneme)	Most Common Spelling Patterns (graphemes)	Tagalog Sound (phoneme) transfer?	Tagalog Spelling pattern (grapheme) transfer?	Korean Sound (phoneme) transfer?	Korean Spelling pattern (grapheme) transfer?	Cantonese Sound (phoneme) transfer?	Cantonese Spelling pattern (grapheme) transfer?	Mandarin Sound (phoneme) transfer?	Mandarin Spelling pattern (grapheme) transfer?	Farsi Sound (phoneme) transfer?	Farsi Spelling pattern (grapheme) transfer?	Arabic Sound (phoneme) transfer?	Arabic Spelling pattern (grapheme) transfer?
/h/	h_	yes	no	yes	no	yes	no	no	no	yes	no	yes	no
/j/	j	no	no	approx.	no	approx.	no	no	no	yes	no	yes	no
	ge		no		no		no		no		no		no
	gi_		no		no		no		no		no		no
	gy		no		no		no		no		no		no
	_dge		no		no		no		no		no		no
	du		no		no		no		no		no		no
	di		no		no		no		no		no		no
/l/	l	yes	yes	yes	no	yes	no	yes	no	yes	no	yes	no
	ll		no		no		no		no		no		no
	-el		no		no		no		no		no		no
	_le		no		no		no		no		no		no
/m/	m	yes	yes	yes	no	yes	no	yes	no	yes	no	yes	no
	mn		no		no		no		no		no		no

©2018 Benchmark Education Company, LLC

Contrastive Analysis of English and Nine World Languages

Sound-Spelling: Consonants

	Sound (phoneme)	Most Common Spelling Patterns (graphemes)	Notes	Word Examples			Spanish Sound (phoneme) transfer?	Spanish Spelling pattern (grapheme) transfer?	Vietnamese Sound (phoneme) transfer?	Vietnamese Spelling pattern (grapheme) transfer?	Hmong Sound (phoneme) transfer?	Hmong Spelling pattern (grapheme) transfer?
The sound /m/ is used or approximated in all of these languages, and the common spelling used to communicate /m/ is m among the alphabetic languages. *continued*	/m/	lm	Low frequency. Some regions do pronounce the l separately.		alms	calm		no		no		no
		mb	Low frequency. When adding affixes, can "cause" both letters to be pronounced (i.e., crumb --> crumble)		climber	lamb		no		no		no
The sound /n/ is used or approximated in most of these languages, and the common spelling used to communicate /n/ is n among the alphabetic languages.	/n/	n	Subject to consonant doubling (inn, connect)	nest	pants	fan	yes	yes	yes	yes	yes	yes
		kn_		knee				no		no		no
		gn	Initial Anglo-Saxon consonant blend that lost "g" sound over time, German, Scandinavian, Latin, Greek	gnome	designing	reign, assign, foreign		no		no		
		pn	Consonant blend in Greek words that "lost" /p/ sound across languages	pneu-monia				no		no		
The sound /p/ is used or approximated in most of these languages, and the common spelling used to communicate /p/ is p among the alphabetic languages.	/p/	p	subject to medial consonant doubling	paper	steps (happy)	help	yes	yes	yes	yes	approx.	yes
The sound /n/ is used or approximated in few of these languages.	/kw/	qu_		queen	liquid		yes	no	yes	yes	no	no
The sound /r/ is used or approximated in few of these languages. Many of these languages use a trilled version of /r/ that is not used in English (e.g., Spanish carro).	/r/	r	subject to medial consonant doubling	radio	carpet (arrow)	star	approx.	yes	approx.	no	no	no
		wr_		write	unwrap			no		no		no
		re	French, British low frequency			acre, theatre		no		no		no
		er, ur, ir (r-controlled vowels)	Syllables where /r/ is the sound requiring a vowel. Frequently misspelled without the vowel.	ermine, herbal, urgent, irk	interest	wonder, fir, fur				no		no
		rh	Greek words	rhyme	hemor-rhage			yes		no		no
		ear (r-controlled)		earth	learn			no		no		no
The sound /s/ is used or approximated in all of these languages, and the common spelling used to communicate /s/ is s among most of the alphabetic languages.	/s/	s		sun	past	gas	yes	yes	yes	yes	yes	no
		ss	Consonant team at the end of a root or last syllable after a short vowel (not a suffix)		lesson	bless, toss, pass		no		no		no
		se	At the end of word or syllable	horse		else, goose		no		no		no
		ce	"Soft c" /s/ when followed by e	cereal	paced	face		yes		yes		no
		ci_	"Soft c" /s/ when followed by i (very rarely at the end of a word, e.g. foci)	circle	incite, incident			yes		yes		no
		cy		cycle, cyst	bicycle	racy		no		no		no

AR54 Additional Resources

©2018 Benchmark Education Company, LLC

Contrastive Analysis of English and Nine World Languages

Sound (phoneme)	Most Common Spelling Patterns (graphemes)	Tagalog Sound (phoneme) transfer?	Tagalog Spelling pattern (grapheme) transfer?	Korean Sound (phoneme) transfer?	Korean Spelling pattern (grapheme) transfer?	Cantonese Sound (phoneme) transfer?	Cantonese Spelling pattern (grapheme) transfer?	Mandarin Sound (phoneme) transfer?	Mandarin Spelling pattern (grapheme) transfer?	Farsi Sound (phoneme) transfer?	Farsi Spelling pattern (grapheme) transfer?	Arabic Sound (phoneme) transfer?	Arabic 'fer?
/m/	lm		no		no		no		no		no		no
	mb		no		no		no		no		no		no
/n/	n		yes		no		no		no		no		no
	kn_		no		no				no		no		no
	gn	no	no	yes		yes	no	yes	no	yes	no	yes	no
	pn		no				no		no		no		no
/p/	p	yes	yes	yes	no	yes	no	yes	no	yes	no	no	no
/kw/	qu_	no	no	yes	no	approx.	no	no	no	no	no	no	no
/r/	r		yes		no		no		no		no		no
	wr_		no		no		no		no		no		no
	re		no		no		no		no		no		no
	er, ur, ir (r-controlled vowels)	yes	no	no	no	no	no	no	no	no	no	no	no
	rh		no		no		no		no		no		no
	ear (r-controlled)		no		no		no		no		no		no
/s/	s		yes		no		no		no		no		no
	ss		no		no		no		no		no		no
	se	yes	no	yes	no	yes	no	yes	no	yes	no	yes	no
	ce		no		no		no		no		no		no
	ci_		no		no		no		no		no		no
	cy		no		no		no		no		no		no

©2018 Benchmark Education Company, LLC

Sound-Spelling: Consonants

	Sound (phoneme)	Most Common Spelling Patterns (graphemes)	Notes	Word Examples			Spanish Sound (phoneme) transfer?	Spanish Spelling pattern (grapheme) transfer?	Vietnamese Sound (phoneme) transfer?	Vietnamese Spelling pattern (grapheme) transfer?	Hmong Sound (phoneme) transfer?	Hmong Spelling pattern (grapheme) transfer?
The sound /s/ *continued*	/s/	sc		scene, science	descend, disciple			no		no		no
		ss	used at the end of a root or last syllable after a short vowel (not a suffix)		assess	grass, princess		no		no		no
The sound /t/ is used or approximated in all of these languages, and the common spelling used to communicate /t/ is t among most of the alphabetic languages.	/t/	t	initial, medial, and final sounds	telephone	after	just, wheat, late	approx.	yes	yes	yes	approx.	no
		tt			bitten, battle	mitt		no		no		no
		_ed	suffix			raced		no		no		no
		pt	few words of Greek origin	pterodactyl				no		no		no
		te, tte	French origin			suite, gazette		no		no		no
The sound /v/ is used or approximated in few of these languages.	/v/	v		van	flavor		no	no	yes	yes	yes	yes
		ve	Word or syllable endings; never end in solo v.		driven	give, brave		no		no		no
The sound /w/ is used or approximated in some of these languages.	/w/	w	Note that many vowel sounds are changed when following w.	Washington	away	cow	yes	approx.	no	no	no	no
The unvoiced sound /hw/ is not used or approximated in any of these languages.	/hw/	wh	Old English beginning of word or syllable. Many question words or whistling/whining sounds. Modern day /w/	why, whale	nowhere		no	no	no	no	no	no
The sound /ks/ is not used or approximated in a few of these languages.	/ks/	_x	Preceded by vowel. Latin prefix ex-. Distinguish between plurals and words (tax vs. tacks)		extra	fix	yes	yes	no	no	no	no
		-cks	plural			ducks		no		no		no
The sound /y/ is used or approximated in most of these languages, but the spelling used to communicate /y/ varies.	/y/	y_	Y is a consonant letter at the beginning of a word or syllable. Any other placement is a vowel.	yucca	lawyer		yes	yes	no	no	yes	yes
The sound /z/ is used, or approximated in some of these languages but the spelling is not the same in the alphabetic languages.	/z/	z	subject to medial consonant doubling	zip	lazy (puzzle)		no	no	yes	no	yes	no
		ze	at the end of a word or syllable			ooze, haze		no		no		no
		_s	sm at the end of syllable or word, between 2 vowels, few HFWs (his, is, was, as, has). Suffix after vowel.		laser, prism	has, lens, bees, days		no		no		no
		_se	long vowel pattern with s (rise). Suffix after s, z, ch, sh			cheese, wise, passes, gazes, coaches, wishes		no		no		no
		s contractions				it's, she's he's		no		no		no
		x	at the beginning of a word	xylophone				no		no		no

AR56 Additional Resources

©2018 Benchmark Education Company, LLC

Contrastive Analysis of English and Nine World Languages

Sound (phoneme)	Most Common Spelling Patterns (graphemes)	Tagalog		Korean		Cantonese		Mandarin		Farsi		Arabic	
		Sound (phoneme) transfer?	Spelling pattern (grapheme) transfer?	Sound (phoneme) transfer?	Spelling pattern (grapheme) transfer?	Sound (phoneme) transfer?	Spelling pattern (grapheme) transfer?	Sound (phoneme) transfer?	Spelling pattern (grapheme) transfer?	Sound (phoneme) transfer?	Spelling pattern (grapheme) transfer?	Sound (phoneme) transfer?	Spelling pattern (grapheme) transfer?
/s/	sc		no		no		no		no		no		no
	ss		no		no		no		no		no		no
/t/	t	yes	yes	yes	no	yes	no	yes	no	yes	no	yes	no
	tt		no		no		no		no		no		no
	_ed		no		no		no		no		no		no
	pt		no		no		no		no		no		no
	te, tte		no		no		no		no		no		
/v/	v	no	no	no	no	no	no	no	no	yes	no	no	no
	ve		no		no		no		no		no		no
/w/	w	yes	yes	yes	no	yes	no	no	no	no	no	yes	no
/hw/	wh	no	no	no	no	no	no	no	no	no	no	no	no
/ks/	_x	no	no	yes	no	no	no	no	no	no	no	no	no
	-cks		no		no		no		no		no		no
/y/	y_	yes	yes	yes	no	yes	no	no	no	yes	no	yes	no
/z/	z	no	no	no	no	no	no	no	no	yes	no	yes	no
	ze		no		no		no		no		no		no
	_s		no		no		no		no		no		no
	_se		no		no		no		no		no		no
	s contractions		no		no		no		no		no		no
	x		no		no		no		no		no		no

©2018 Benchmark Education Company, LLC

Contrastive Analysis of English and Nine World Languages

Sound-Spelling: Consonant Digraphs

Sound (phoneme)	Most Common Spelling Patterns (graphemes)	Notes	Word Examples			Spanish		Vietnamese		Hmong	
						Sound (phoneme) transfer?	Spelling pattern (grapheme) transfer?	Sound (phoneme) transfer?	Spelling pattern (grapheme) transfer?	Sound (phoneme) transfer?	Spelling pattern (grapheme) transfer?
			initial	medial	final						
/ch/	ch		chile	satchel	inch	yes	yes	yes	no	no	no
	_tch	Used after short vowel in root.		hatchet	crutch		no		no		no
	tu	Latin origin. Unstressed long u impacts the /t/ sound.		culture, situate, fortunate, mutual			no		no		no
	ci, ce	Small number of foreign words commonly used in English	cello	concerto, ancient, financial			no		no		no
/sh/	sh		sheep	ashes	wish	no	no	yes	no	no	no
	ch	French words	chef, chic	machine	mustache		no		no		no
	ci	Latin (-cial, -scious, -cious)		social, efficient			no		no		no
	ti			nation, patience, initial			no		no		no
	ssi	Latin, unstressed i before a vowel. Adding /shun/ after ss.		passion, (express) expression			no		no		no
	-su-	Usually sh sound, sometimes /zh/	sure	insure, pressure			no		no		no
	si	Latin. Unstressed i before a vowel.		mansion, tension			no		no		no
/hw/	wh_		when	nowhere		no	no	no	no	no	
/th/ (voiced)	th	Native English words, most in beginning reader level words. Often "pointing" words (this, there, thy, thee, theirs)	these	feather	bathe, smooth	approx.	no	no	no	no	

AR58 Additional Resources

©2018 Benchmark Education Company, LLC

Contrastive Analysis of English and Nine World Languages

Sound (phoneme)	Most Common Spelling Patterns (graphemes)	Tagalog Sound (phoneme) transfer?	Tagalog Spelling pattern (grapheme) transfer?	Korean Sound (phoneme) transfer?	Korean Spelling pattern (grapheme) transfer?	Cantonese Sound (phoneme) transfer?	Cantonese Spelling pattern (grapheme) transfer?	Mandarin Sound (phoneme) transfer?	Mandarin Spelling pattern (grapheme) transfer?	Farsi Sound (phoneme) transfer?	Farsi Spelling pattern (grapheme) transfer?	Arabic Sound (phoneme) transfer?	Arabic Spelling pattern (grapheme) transfer?
/ch/	ch	yes	no	no	no	no	no	approx.	no	yes	no	no	no
	_tch		no		no		no		no		no		no
	tu		no		no		no		no		no		no
	ci, ce		no		no		no		no		no		no
/sh/	sh	yes	yes	no	no	no	no	approx.	no	no	no	yes	no
	ch		no		no		no		no		no		no
	ci		no		no		no		no		no		no
	ti		no		no		no		no		no		no
	ssi		no		no		no		no		no		no
	-su-		no		no		no		no		no		no
	si		no		no		no		no		no		no
/hw/	wh_	no	no		no	no	no	no	no	no	no	no	no
/th/ (voiced)	th	no	no		no	no	no	no	no	no	no	yes	no

©2018 Benchmark Education Company, LLC

Contrastive Analysis of English and Nine World Languages

Sound-Spelling: Consonant Digraphs

Sound (phoneme)	Most Common Spelling Patterns (graphemes)	Notes	Word Examples			Spanish Sound (phoneme) transfer?	Spanish Spelling pattern (grapheme) transfer?	Vietnamese Sound (phoneme) transfer?	Vietnamese Spelling pattern (grapheme) transfer?	Hmong Sound (phoneme) transfer?	Hmong Spelling pattern (grapheme) transfer?
/th/ (un-voiced)	th	At the begin-ning of nouns, verbs, adjec-tives. In Greek words between vowels. Beyond children's book words, most are unvoiced.	think	panther	math	approx.	no	no	no		no
/ng/	ng (a few exceptions such as tongue)			mango	hang	yes	yes	yes	yes		no
	n (followed by /k/)		uncle, conquer, sphinx	thank			no		no		no
/zh/	-si-	/s/ changed to /zh/ when followed by un-sressed i before a vowel			vision, division, version	no	no	partial	no		no
	ge, gi	French "soft g" before e, I, y	gendarme	regime	garage		no		no		no
	-su-	Usually sh sound		usual, visual, closure			no		no		no
	z	Unstressed I or long u before vowel		azure, brazier			no		no		no
/gz/	ex	When syllable ending in x is unstressed and the next syllable begins with a vowel or silent h	exhaust, exact	unexampled		no	no	no	no		no

AR60 Additional Resources

©2018 Benchmark Education Company, LLC

Contrastive Analysis of English and Nine World Languages

Sound (phoneme)	Most Common Spelling Patterns (graphemes)	Tagalog		Korean		Cantonese		Mandarin		Farsi		Arabic	
		Sound (phoneme) transfer?	Spelling pattern (grapheme) transfer?	Sound (phoneme) transfer?	Spelling pattern (grapheme) transfer?	Sound (phoneme) transfer?	Spelling pattern (grapheme) transfer?	Sound (phoneme) transfer?	Spelling pattern (grapheme) transfer?	Sound (phoneme) transfer?	Spelling pattern (grapheme) transfer?	Sound (phoneme) transfer?	Spelling pattern (grapheme) transfer?
/th/ (un-voiced)	th	no	no		no	no	no	no	no	no	no	yes	no
/ng/	ng (a few exceptions such as tongue)	yes	yes		no	yes	no	yes	no	no	no	no	no
	n (followed by /k/)	yes	no		no	yes	no	yes	no	no	no	no	no
/zh/	-si-	no	no		no	no	no	no	no	no	no	no	no
	ge, gi	no	no		no	no	no	no	no	no	no	no	no
	-su-	no	no		no	no	no	no	no	no	no	no	no
	z	no	no		no	no	no	no	no	no	no	no	no
/gz/	ex	no	no		no	no	no	no	no		no		no

©2018 Benchmark Education Company, LLC

Contrastive Analysis of English and Nine World Languages

Sound-Spelling: Short and Long Vowels

Short Vowels

Sound (phoneme)	Most Common Spelling Patterns (graphemes)	Notes	initial	medial	final	Spanish Sound (phoneme) transfer?	Spanish Spelling pattern (grapheme) transfer?	Vietnamese Sound (phoneme) transfer?	Vietnamese Spelling pattern (grapheme) transfer?	Hmong Sound (phoneme) transfer?	Hmong Spelling pattern (grapheme) transfer?
/ā/	a	closed syllables	apple	cab		no	no	approx.	yes	yes	yes
/ĕ/	e	closed syllables	egg	pet		yes	yes	approx.	yes	no	no
/ĭ/	i	closed syllables	igloo	bit		no	no	no	no	no	no
/ŏ/	o	closed syllables	octopus	rock		no	no	approx.	yes	approx.	yes
/ŏ/	ough			ought	bought				no		no
/ŏ/	augh			aught	daughter, caught				no		no
/ŭ/	u	closed syllables	under	munch		no	no	yes	no	no	no

Long Vowels

Sound (phoneme)	Spelling pattern	Notes	initial	medial	final	Spanish Sound transfer?	Spanish Spelling transfer?	Vietnamese Sound transfer?	Vietnamese Spelling transfer?	Hmong Sound transfer?	Hmong Spelling transfer?
/ā/	a	open syllable	able	caper		yes	no	approx.	no	approx.	no
	ai_		aim	stair			no		no		no
	_ay				stay		no		no		no
	a_e		ale	baseball	paste		no		no		no
	eigh		eight	neighbor	weigh		no		no		no
/ē/	e	open syllable	ether	defend	me	yes	no	yes	no	yes	no
	ee			seed	knee		no		no		no
	ea		east	wheat			no		no		no
	e_e		*eke		these		no		no		no
	_y				happy		no		no		no
	_ie_						no		no		no
	igh			light	sigh		no		no		no
/ī/	i	open syllable	item	bicycle	*hi	yes	no	yes	no	yes	no
	i_e		ice	tired	bik1		no		no		no
	_y			myself	fly		no		no		no
	igh			bright	high		no		no		no
	_ie				tie		no		no		no
/ō/	o	open syllable	open	motor		yes	yes	approx.	no	no	no
	oa		oath	boat			no		no		no
	_oe				toe		no		no		no
	ow				bow		no		no		no
	o_e		ode		globe		no		no		no
	ough	low frequency			though				no		no
/ū/	u	open syllable	unicorn	cucumber		yes	no	no	no	no	no
	_ue				rescue		no		no		no
	u_e				cube		no		no		no
	_ew				few		no		no		no

AR62 Additional Resources

©2018 Benchmark Education Company, LLC

Contrastive Analysis of English and Nine World Languages

Sound (phoneme)	Most Common Spelling Patterns (graphemes)	Tagalog Sound (phoneme) transfer?	Tagalog Spelling pattern (grapheme) transfer?	Korean Sound (phoneme) transfer?	Korean Spelling pattern (grapheme) transfer?	Cantonese Sound (phoneme) transfer?	Cantonese Spelling pattern (grapheme) transfer?	Mandarin Sound (phoneme) transfer?	Mandarin Spelling pattern (grapheme) transfer?	Farsi Sound (phoneme) transfer?	Farsi Spelling pattern (grapheme) transfer?	Arabic Sound (phoneme) transfer?	Arabic Spelling pattern (grapheme) transfer?
/ā/	a	no	no	yes	no	no	no	no	no	approx.	no	approx.	no
/ĕ/	e	yes	no	yes	no	approx.	no	approx.	no	approx.	no	approx.	no
/ĭ/	i	no	no	yes	no	approx.	no	approx.	no		no	approx.	no
/ŏ/	o	no	no	approx.	no	approx.	no	approx.	no	approx.	no	approx.	no
/ŏ/	ough		no		no		no		no		no		no
/ŏ/	augh		no		no		no		no		no		no
/ū/	u	yes	no	no	no	approx.	no	approx.	no	no	no	yes	no

Sound (phoneme)	graphemes	Tagalog Sound	Tagalog Spelling	Korean Sound	Korean Spelling	Cantonese Sound	Cantonese Spelling	Mandarin Sound	Mandarin Spelling	Farsi Sound	Farsi Spelling	Arabic Sound	Arabic Spelling
/ā/	a	no	no	yes	no	approx.	no	approx.	no	yes	no	yes	no
/ā/	ai_		no		no		no		no		no		no
/ā/	_ay		no		no		no		no		no		no
/ā/	a_e		no		no		no		no		no		no
/ā/	eigh		no		no		no		no		no		no
/ē/	e	yes	no	yes	no	approx.	no	yes	no	yes	no	yes	no
/ē/	ee		no		no		no		no		no		no
/ē/	ea		no		no		no		no		no		no
/ē/	e_e		no		no		no		no		no		no
/ē/	_y		no		no		no		no		no		no
/ē/	_ie_		no		no		no		no		no		no
/ē/	igh		no		no		no		no		no		no
/ī/	i	no	no	yes	no	approx.	no	approx.	no	no	no	approx.	no
/ī/	i_e		no		no		no		no		no		no
/ī/	_y		no		no		no		no		no		no
/ī/	igh		no		no		no		no		no		no
/ī/	_ie		no		no		no		no		no		no
/ō/	o	yes	no	yes	no	approx.	no	approx.	no	approx.	no	no	no
/ō/	oa		no		no		no		no		no		no
/ō/	_oe		no		no		no		no		no		no
/ō/	ow		no		no		no		no		no		no
/ō/	o_e		no		no		no		no		no		no
/ō/	ough		no		no		no		no		no		no
/ū/	u	no	no	yes	no	approx.	no	approx.	no	no	no	no	no
/ū/	_ue		no		no		no		no		no		no
/ū/	u_e		no		no		no		no		no		no
/ū/	_ew		no		no		no		no		no		no

©2018 Benchmark Education Company, LLC

Contrastive Analysis of English and Nine World Languages

Sound-Spelling: R-Controlled Vowels, Other Vowel Patterns

		English				Spanish		Vietnamese		Hmong	
			initial	**medial**	**final**						
R-Controlled Vowels	/är/	ar	arm	barn	far	approx.**	yes	no	no	no	no
	/ûr/	er	ernest	fern	teacher	no	no	no	no	no	no
		ir	irk	girl	fir		no		no		no
		ur	urn	curl	fur		no		no		no
		ear	early,	pearl			*no*		*no*		*no*
			initial	**medial**	**final**						
Other Vowel Patterns	/oi/	oi	oil	broil		yes	yes	approx.	yes	no	no
		_oy	*oyster		boy		yes		no		no
	/ou/	ow	owl	brown	how	no	yes	yes	no	approx.	no
		ou_	out	cloud		no			no		no
	/ô/	aw	awful	crawl	draw	approx.	no	yes	no	approx.	no
		au_	augment				no		no		no
	/ôl/	al	also			approx.	yes	yes	no	no	no
		all	all		hall		no		no		no
		ol		follow			no		no		no
		awl	crawl				no		no		no
	/ōō/	oo	ooze	moon	boo	yes	no	yes	no	yes	no
		u_e	ruler				no		yes		yes
		_ew	flew				no		no		no
		_ue	blue				no		no		yes
		ui	suit				*no*		*no*		*yes*
		ough			through		*no*		*no*		*no*
	/oo/	oo		book		no	no	approx.	no	no	no

AR64 Additional Resources

©2018 Benchmark Education Company, LLC

Contrastive Analysis of English and Nine World Languages

		Tagalog		Korean		Cantonese		Mandarin		Farsi		Arabic	
R-Controlled Vowels	/är/	no	no	no	no	no	no	no	no	no	no	no	no
	/ûr/	no		no	no	approx.	no	approx.	no	no	no	no	no
					no		no		no		no		no
			no		no		no		no		no		no
			no		*no*		*no*		*no*		*no*		*no*
Other Vowel Patterns	/oi/	yes	no	yes	no	approx.	no	no	no	no	no	no	no
			no		no		no		no		no		no
	/ou/	no		yes	no	approx.	no	approx.	no	yes		no	no
			no		no		no		no		no		no
	/ô/	yes	no	approx.	no	yes	no	no	no	no	no	no	no
					no		no		no		no		no
	/ôl/	yes	no	approx.	no	approx.	no	no	no	no	no	no	no
			no		no		no		no		no		no
			no		no		no		no		no		no
			no		no		no		no		no		no
	/o͞o/	yes	no	yes	no	approx.	no	yes	no	yes	no	yes	no
			no		no		no		no		no		no
			no		no		no		no		no		no
			no		no		no		no		no		no
			no		no		no		no		no		*no*
			no		no		no		no		no		*no*
	/oo/	no	no	approx.	no	approx.	no	approx.	no	no	no	no	no

©2018 Benchmark Education Company, LLC

Additional Resources **AR65**

Contrastive Analysis of English and Nine World Languages

Syntax and Grammar: Verbs

Differences and Potential Errors for English Learners

English Grammar	Spanish	Vietnamese	Hmong	Tagalog
VERBS				
Use of **infinitives*** *(He wants them to learn quickly.)*	Clause "that" is used rather than an infinitive *(He wants that they learn quickly.)*		Clause "that" is used rather than an infinitive *(He wants that they learn quickly.)*	
Use of **infinitives to express** purpose *(We go out to have dinner.)*				
Verbs are separated with punctuation or other words *(I throw, catch, and kick the ball).*		Verbs can be used together without punctuation or other words *(I throw catch kick the ball.)*	Verbs can be used together without punctuation or other words (I throw catch kick the ball.)	
Use of **gerund**** (-ing) /infinitive distinction). *(She enjoys cooking.)*	No use of gerund (-ing)/ infinitive distinction. *(She enjoys to cook.)*	No use of gerund (-ing)/ infinitive distinction. *(She enjoys to cook.)*	No use of gerund (-ing)/ infinitive distinction. (She enjoys to cook.)	
Use of the **verb "to be"** *(He is walking. They are coming to school.).*		Be can be omitted. *(He walking. They coming to school.)*	Be can be omitted. *(He walking. They coming to school.)*	Be can be omitted. *(He walking. They coming to school.)*
Use of the verb "to be" for adjectives or places *(The lock is strong. The book is on the desk.)*		The verb "to be" is not used for adjectives or places *(The lock strong. The book on the desk.)*	The verb "to be" is not used for adjectives or places *(The lock strong. The book on the desk.)*	The verb "to be" is not used for adjectives or places *(The lock strong. The book on the desk.)*
Use of the **verb "to be" to express states of being** such as hunger or age).	The verb "to have" can be used to express states of being (age, hunger, etc.). She *has* ten years. They *have* hunger.			
Use of **"there is/are,was/ were"** *(In school, there are many students.")*	Can use "have" *(In school they have many students.)* or "there are" *(In school, there are many students.)*	Use of "have" instead of "there is/ are,was/were" *(In school, have many students.")*	Use of "have" instead of "there is/ are,was/were" *(In school, have many students.")*	
Change in verb "to be" in past perfect form. *(They are climbing --> They climbed).*				
Use of **verb "to have"** *(I have one book.)*				
Verb inflection for person and number. *(Everyone cooks food. She has a large cat.)*		Verbs are not inflected for person and number. *(Everyone cook food. She have a large cat.)*	Verbs are not inflected for person and number. *(Everyone cook food. She have a large cat.)*	
Verb tenses change within the same sentence. *(When we eat, we will be full.)*			Verb tenses do not change within the same sentence. *(When we eat, we full.)*	
Use of **tense boundaries** *(I will study here for a year. When she was young, she played with dolls.)*		Tense can be indicated by context or an expression of time rather than through the verb tense. *(I study here for a year. When she is young, she play with dolls.)*	Tense indicated by use of infinitive of verb with an expression of time rather than through the verb tense.	
Use of **future tense** *(I will go tomorrow)* and **present perfect** tense *(I have been there many times).*	Present tense can replace future tense *(I go there tomorrow)* and can replace present perfect *(I go there many times).*		Present tense can replace future tense *(I go there tomorrow)* and can replace present perfect *(I go there many times).*	
Use of **passive tense** *(Their window was broken.)*		Different limits for use of passive tense *(They were broken their window.)*		

*An infinitive can be considered the "base verb" that can be conjugated into different forms to represent past, present, future (e.g., to run, to sing, to eat, to be).

**A gerund is a verb that functions as a noun in a sentence. Gerunds end in -ing (e.g., Running is great exercise). In this sentence, the verb (in infinitive form) to run is functioning as a noun and the verb is (conjugated from the infinitive to be) functions as the verb.

AR66   Additional Resources

©2018 Benchmark Education Company, LLC

Contrastive Analysis of English and Nine World Languages

Common Core Language Standard 1:
Demonstrate command of the conventions of standard English grammar and usage when writing or speaking.

L.K.1b Use frequently occurring nouns and verbs.
L.1.1e Use verbs to convey a sense of past, present, and future.
L.2.1d Form and use the past tense of frequently occurring irregular verbs.
L.3.1d Form and use regular and irregular verbs.
L.3.1e Form and use the simple verb tenses.

L.4.1b Form and use the progressive verb tenses.
L.4.1c Use modal auxiliaries to convey various conditions.
L.5.1b Form and use the perfect verb tenses.
L.5.1c Use verb tense to convey various times, sequences, states, and conditions.
L.5.1d Recognize and correct inappropriate shifts in verb tense.*

English Grammar	Korean	Cantonese	Mandarin	Farsi	Arabic
VERBS					
Use of **infinitives*** *(He wants them to learn quickly.)*					
Use of **infinitives to express** purpose *(We go out to have dinner.)*	Infinitives not used to express purpose *(We go out for having dinner.)*				
Verbs are separated with punctuation or other words *(I throw, catch, and kick the ball).*					
Use of **gerund**** (-ing) /infinitive distinction). *(She enjoys cooking.)*	No use of gerund (-ing)/ infinitive distinction. *(She enjoys to cook.)*	No use of gerund (-ing)/ infinitive distinction. *(She enjoys to cook.)*	No use of gerund (-ing)/ infinitive distinction. *(She enjoys to cook.)* Tense is expressed by adding adverbs of time instead of changing the verb form.	No use of gerund (-ing)/ infinitive distinction. *(She enjoys to cook.)*	No use of gerund (-ing)/ infinitive distinction. *(She enjoys to cook.)*
Use of the **verb "to be"** *(He is walking. They are coming to school.)*	Be can be omitted. *(He walking. They coming to school.)*	Be can be omitted. *(He walking. They coming to school.)* Tense is expressed by adding adverbs of time instead of changing the verb form.	Be can be omitted. *(He walking. They coming to school.)* Adjectives an be directly used as verbs.		Be can be omitted. *(He walking. They coming to school.)*
Use of the verb "to be" for adjectives or places *(The lock is strong. The book is on the desk.)*					
Use of the **verb "to be"** to **express states of being** such as hunger or age).				The verb "to have" can be used to express states of being (age, hunger, etc.). She *has* ten years. They *have* hunger.	
Use of **"there is/are,was/ were"** (*In school, there are many students."*)					
Change in verb "to be" in past perfect form. *(They are climbing --> They climbed).*				Past perfect form for "to be" changes differently. *(They are climbing --> They were climbed.)*	Past perfect form for "to be" changes differently. *(They are climbing --> They were climbed.)*
Use of **verb "to have"** *(I have one book.)*	The verb "to have" can be substituted with "to be" *(I am book.)*				
Verb inflection for person and number. *(Everyone cooks food. She has a large cat.)*	Verbs are not inflected for person and number. *(Everyone cook food. She have a large cat.)* In Korean verbs are inflected for age or status.	Verbs are not inflected for person and number. *(Everyone cook food. She have a large cat.)*	Verbs are not inflected for person and number. *(Everyone cook food. She have a large cat.)*		
Verb tenses change within the same sentence. *(When we eat, we will be full.)*					
Use of **tense boundaries** (*I will study here for a year. When she was young, she played with dolls.*)		Tense can be indicated by context or an expression of time rather than through the verb tense. *(I study here for a year. When she is young, she play with dolls.)*	Tense can be indicated by context or an expression of time rather than through the verb tense. *(I study here for a year. When she is young, she play with dolls.)*		Tense can be indicated by context or an expression of time rather than through the verb tense. *(I study here for a year. When she is young, she play with dolls.)*
Use of **future tense** *(I will go tomorrow)* and **present perfect** tense *(I have been there many times).*				Present tense can replace future tense *(I go there tomorrow)* and can replace present perfect *(I go there many times).*	
Use of **passive tense** *(Their window was broken.)*	Different limits for use of passive tense *(They were broken their window.)*				Different limits for use of passive tense (They were broken their window.)

©2018 Benchmark Education Company, LLC

Additional Resources **AR67**

Contrastive Analysis of English and Nine World Languages

Syntax and Grammar: Nouns
Differences and Potential Errors for English Learners

English Grammar	Spanish	Vietnamese	Hmong	Tagalog
NOUNS				
Nouns and adjectives use different forms *(They felt safe in their home.)*	Suffixes can be added to nouns (e.g. -ito, -oso) to combine description with a noun.		Nouns and adjectives can use the same form *(They felt safety in their home.)*	
Nouns and verbs are distinct.			Nouns and verbs may not be distinct.	Nouns and verbs may not be distinct.
Use of **proper names** in first, middle, last order *(George Lucas Smith).*		Proper names can be ordered in last, first, middle order or last, middle, first. First and last names can be confusing to teachers and students.	Proper names can be ordered in last, first, middle order, or last, middle, first. First and last names can be confusing to teachers and students.	Depends on familiarity.
Use of 's for **possessive nouns** *(This is Holly's box.)*	Possessive nouns are formed with an "of phase" (This is the box of Holly.)	Possessive nouns are formed with an "of phase" (This is the box of Holly.)	Possessive nouns are formed with an "of phase" (This is the box of Holly.)	Possessive nouns are formed with an "of phase" (This is the box of Holly.)
Use of **plural nouns** *(She makes many friends. He has few questions.)*		No use of plural nouns *(She make many friend. He has few question.)* Plurals can be expressed through an adjective quantifier.	No use of plural nouns *(He has few question.)* Plurals are used for nouns related to people such as "friends." Plurals can be expressed through an adjective quantifier.	No use of plural nouns *(She make many friend. He has few question.)* Plurals can be expressed through an adjective quantifier.
Use of **plural forms** after a number *(We go home in two weeks. They are bringing five shirts.)*		Use of plural forms after a number *(We go home in two week. They are bringing five shirt.)*	Use of plural forms after a number *(We go home in two week. They are bringing five shirt.)*	Use of plural forms after a number *(We go home in two week. They are bringing five shirt.)*
Use of -es to make **plural nouns** only used after nouns ending in consonants s, x, ch, sh, and z. *(passes, foxes, catches, wishes, buzzes)* Nouns ending in y change the y to i before adding -es. *(candies)*	Use of -es to make plural nouns for all nouns that end in consonants or y (walls --> walles, pay --> payes)			
Use of **noncount nouns** that do not have plurals such as *weather, homework, money, rain,* etc. *(We have different types of weather. We have a lot of homework.)*		Confusion with noncount nouns that do not have plurals *(We have different types of weathers. We have a lot of homeworks.)*	Confusion with noncount nouns that do not have plurals *(We have different types of weathers. We have a lot of homeworks.)*	Confusion with noncount nouns that do not have plurals *(We have different types of weathers. We have a lot of homeworks.)*

AR68   Additional Resources

©2018 Benchmark Education Company, LLC

Contrastive Analysis of English and Nine World Languages

Common Core Language Standard 1:

Demonstrate command of the conventions of standard English grammar and usage when writing or speaking.

L.K.1b Use frequently occurring nouns and verbs.
L.K.1c Form regular plural nouns orally by adding /s/ or /es/ (e.g., dog, dogs; wish, wishes).
L.1.1b Use common, proper, and possessive nouns.
L.1.1c Use singular and plural nouns with matching verbs in basic sentences (e.g., He hops; We hop).
L.2.1a Use collective nouns (e.g., group).
L.2.1b Form and use frequently occurring irregular plural nouns (e.g., feet, children, teeth, mice, fish).
L.3.1b Form and use regular and irregular plural nouns.
L.3.1c Use abstract nouns (e.g., childhood).

English Grammar	Korean	Cantonese	Mandarin	Farsi	Arabic
NOUNS					
Nouns and adjectives use different forms *(They felt safe in their home.)*		Nouns and adjectives can use the same form *(They felt safety in their home.)*	Nouns and adjectives can use the same form *(They felt safety in their home.)*		
Nouns and verbs are distinct.		Nouns and verbs overlap, may not be distinct.	Nouns and verbs overlap, may not be distinct.	Nouns and verbs may not be distinct.	
Use of **proper names** in first, middle, last order *(George Lucas Smith).*	Proper names can be ordered in last, first, middle order, or last, middle, first. First and last names can be confusing to teachers and students.	Proper names can be ordered in last, first, middle order, or last, middle, first. First and last names can be confusing to teachers and students. (Chinese: Always last name first)	Proper names can be ordered in last, first, middle order, or last, middle, first. First and last names can be confusing to teachers and students. (Chinese: Always last name first)		
Use of 's for **possessive nouns** *(This is Holly's box.)*		Possessive nouns are consistently formed (Holly's box.)			
Use of **plural nouns** *(She makes many friends. He has few questions.)*	No use of plural nouns *(She make many friend. He has few question.)* Plurals can be expressed through an adjective quantifier. In Korean, nouns related to people (e.g., children) have plural forms, but not other nouns.	No use of plural nouns *(She make many friend. He has few question.)* Plurals can be expressed through an adjective quantifier.	No use of plural nouns *(She make many friend. He has few question.)* Plurals can be expressed through an adjective quantifier or number word.		
Use of **plural forms** after a number *(We go home in two weeks. They are bringing five shirts.)*	Use of plural forms after a number *(We go home in two week. They are bringing five shirt.)* Students may add a word rather than adding -s to a noun.	Use of plural forms after a number *(We go home in two week. They are bringing five shirt.)*	Use of plural forms after a number *(We go home in two week. They are bringing five shirt.)*	Use of plural forms after a number *(We go home in two week. They are bringing five shirt.)*	
Use of -es to make **plural nouns** only used after nouns ending in consonants s, x, ch, sh, and z. *(passes, foxes, catches, wishes, buzzes)* Nouns ending in y change the y to i before adding -es. *(candies)*					
Use of **noncount nouns** that do not have plurals such as *weather, homework, money, rain,* etc. *(We have different types of weather. We have a lot of homework.)*	Confusion with noncount nouns that do not have plurals *(We have different types of weathers. We have a lot of homeworks.)*	Confusion with noncount nouns that do not have plurals *(We have different types of weathers. We have a lot of homeworks.)*	Confusion with noncount nouns that do not have plurals *(We have different types of weathers. We have a lot of homeworks.)*	Confusion with noncount nouns that do not have plurals *(We have different types of weathers. We have a lot of homeworks.)*	

©2018 Benchmark Education Company, LLC

Additional Resources **AR69**

Contrastive Analysis of English and Nine World Languages

Syntax and Grammar:
Word Order and Sentence Structure
Differences and Potential Errors for English Learners

English Grammar	Spanish	Vietnamese	Hmong	Tagalog
WORD ORDER				
Subject-Verb-Object and, Object-Verb-Subject order can be used. *(Every student in the class received good grades. Good grades were received by every student in the class.)*	Word order can change and can change the emphasis.	The usual word order is subject-verb-object.	The usual word order is subject-verb-object.	The word order is subject-verb-object, or object-verb-subject.
Use of subject pronouns *(They are coming. He is running.)*	Optional use of subject pronouns when the subject is understood *(They coming. He running).*	Optional use of subject pronouns when the subject is understood *(They coming. He running).*	Optional use of subject pronouns when the subject is understood *(They coming. He running).*	Optional use of subject pronouns when the subject is understood *(They coming. He running).*
Pronouns used as Indirect objects precede the direct object *(He gave her an umbrella.)*			Direct objects precede pronouns used as Indirect objects *(He gave an umbrella her).*	
Verbs precede adverbs and adverbial phrases *(She runs quickly. They travel to work by train.)*				Adverbs and adverbial phrases precede verbs *(She quickly runs. They by train travel to work).*
Sentences always include a subject. *(Is this your chair? Yes, it is. Is it raining?)*	Sentences do not always include a subject *(Is this your chair? Yes, is. Is raining?)*			
Subjects and verbs can be inverted *(He is cooking and so am I.)*	Verbs can precede subject *(Good grades were received by every student in the class).*		Subjects and verbs are rarely inverted, so one might be deleted or flipped in English *(He is cooking and so am. He is cooking and so I am).*	
Relative clause or restrictive phrase follows a noun it modifies *(The student enrolled in community college.)*				

AR70   Additional Resources

©2018 Benchmark Education Company, LLC

Contrastive Analysis of English and Nine World Languages

Language Standard 1:

Demonstrate command of the conventions of standard English grammar and usage when writing or speaking.

L.K.1d Understand and use question words (interrogatives) (e.g., who, what, where, when, why, how).
L.K.1f Produce and expand complete sentences in shared language activities.
L.1.1c Use singular and plural nouns with matching verbs in basic sentences (e.g., He hops; We hop).
L.1.1j Produce and expand complete simple and compound declarative, interrogative, imperative, and exclamatory sentences in response to prompts.
L.2.1f Produce, expand, and rearrange complete simple and compound sentences (e.g., The boy watched the movie; The little boy watched the movie; The action movie was watched by the little boy).
L.3.1a Explain the function of nouns, pronouns, verbs, adjectives, and adverbs in general and their functions in particular sentences.
L.3.1f Ensure subject-verb and pronoun-antecedent agreement.*
L.3.1i Produce simple, compound, and complex sentences.
L.4.1d Order adjectives within sentences according to conventional patterns (e.g., a small red bag rather than a red small bag).
L.4.1g Correctly use frequently confused words (e.g., to, too, two; there, their).*
L.4.1f Produce complete sentences, recognizing and correcting inappropriate fragments and run-ons.*
L.5.1a Explain the function of conjunctions, prepositions, and interjections in general and their function in particular sentences.

English Grammar	Korean	Cantonese	Mandarin	Farsi	Arabic
WORD ORDER					
Subject-Verb-Object and, Object-Verb-Subject order can be used. *(Every student in the class received good grades. Good grades were received by every student in the class.)*	Verbs are placed last in a sentence. The usual word order is subject-object-verb *(Every student in the class good grades received).*	The most common word order is subject-verb-object but object-subject-verb is used to emphasize the object.	The most common word order is subject-verb-object but object-subject-verb is used to emphasize the object.	Verbs are placed last in a sentence. The usual word order is subject-object-verb *(Every student in the class good grades received.)*	Verbs can precede subject and subject can precede verbs in Arabic. When the subject precedes verb, the sentence is nominative. When the verb precedes subject, the sentence is verbal. *(Good grades received every student in the class.)*
Use of subject pronouns *(They are coming. He is running.)*	Optional use of subject pronouns when the subject is understood *(They coming. He running).* Korean: Can omit the subject pronoun "you."	Optional use of subject pronouns when the subject is understood *(They coming. He running).*	Optional use of subject pronouns when the subject is understood *(They coming. He running.)*	Optional use of subject pronouns when the subject is understood *(They coming. He running.)*	
Pronouns used as Indirect objects precede the direct object *(He gave her an umbrella.)*		Direct objects precede pronouns used as Indirect objects *(He gave an umbrella her).*	Direct objects precede pronouns used as Indirect objects *(He gave an umbrella her).*	Direct objects precede pronouns used as Indirect objects *(He gave an umbrella her.)*	
Verbs precede adverbs and adverbial phrases *(She runs quickly. They travel to work by train.)*	Adverbs and adverbial phrases precede verbs *(She quickly runs. They by train travel to work).*	Adverbs and adverbial phrases precede verbs *(She quickly runs. They by train travel to work).*	Adverbs and adverbial phrases precede verbs *(She quickly runs. They by train travel to work).*	Adverbs and adverbial phrases precede verbs *(She quickly runs. They by train travel to work.)*	Some adverbs can precede or follow verbs. *(Sometimes he studies. He studies sometimes. They travel by train. By train they travel.)*
Sentences always include a subject. *(Is this your chair? Yes, it is. Is it raining?)*					Sentences do not always include a subject *(Is this your chair? Yes, is. Is raining?)*
Subjects and verbs can be inverted *(He is cooking and so am I.)*	Subjects and verbs are rarely inverted, so one might be deleted or flipped in English *(He is cooking and so am. He is cooking and so I am).*	Subjects and verbs are rarely inverted, so one might be deleted or flipped in English *(He is cooking and so am. He is cooking and so I am).*	Subjects and verbs are rarely inverted, so one might be deleted or flipped in English *(He is cooking and so am. He is cooking and so I am).*	Subjects and verbs are rarely inverted, so one might be deleted or flipped in English *(He is cooking and so am. He is cooking and so I am).*	
Relative clause or restrictive phrase follows a noun it modifies *(The student enrolled in community college.)*	Relative clause or restrictive phrase precedes a noun it modifies *(The enrolled in community college student).*	Relative clause or restrictive phrase precedes a noun it modifies *(The enrolled in community college student.)*	Relative clause or restrictive phrase precedes a noun it modifies *(The enrolled in community college student.)*		

©2018 Benchmark Education Company, LLC

Additional Resources **AR71**

Contrastive Analysis of English and Nine World Languages

Syntax and Grammar: Word Order and Sentence Structure
Differences and Potential Errors for English Learners

English Grammar	Spanish	Vietnamese	Hmong	Tagalog
QUESTIONS				
Yes/No questions usually begin with a question word. *(Do you eat broccoli? Is this your sweater?)*	Yes/No questions can be formed by adding an element to the end of a declarative statement. *(You eat broccoli, yes? This is your sweater, no?)*	Yes/No questions can be formed by adding an element to the end of a declarative statement. *(You eat broccoli, yes? This is your sweater, no?)* Vietnamese can also use a statement followed by the phrase: "or not."	Yes/No questions can be formed by adding an element to the end of a declarative statement *(You eat broccoli, yes? This is your sweater, no?)* Yes/No questions can be formed by adding the question word between the pronoun and the verb. (You [question word] take the bus?)	Yes/No questions can be formed by adding an element to the end of a declarative statement *(You eat broccoli, yes? This is your sweater, no?)*
Yes/No questions can be formed by adding a verb followed by its negative at the end of a statement. *(Do you like to go to the beach or not?)*		Yes/No questions can be formed by adding a verb followed by its negative within a statement. *(Do you not like to go to the beach?)*	Yes/No questions can be formed by adding a verb followed by its negative within a statement. *(Do you not like to go to the beach?)*	
Questions words are usually placed at the beginning of the sentence. *(Where is the book? What did my sister tell you?)*		Question words are placed according to the position of the answer. For example, if the answer functions as an object, the question words are placed in the regular object position *(The book is where? My sister told you what?)*	Question words are placed according to the position of the answer. For example, if the answer functions as an object, the question words are placed in the regular object position. *(The book is where? My sister told you what?)*	
Yes and no answers are used in a consistent manner. *(Do you play soccer? Yes. Do you play hockey? No.)*			The answers yes and no vary depending upon the verb used in the question. Students may substitute a verb for a yes-no answer *(Do you play soccer? Soccer. Do you play hockey? No hockey.)*	The answers yes and no vary depending upon the verb used in the question. Students may substitute a verb for a yes-no answer *(Do you play soccer? Soccer. Do you play hockey? No hockey.)*
COMMANDS				
Commands are formed consistently. *(Stop it now!)*		Commands can be formed by adding an adverb after the verbs to be emphasized. *(Stop right now!)* Commands can be formed by adding the verb "go" for emphasis at the end of the sentence. *(Get my slippers, go!)*	Commands can be formed by adding an adverb after the verbs to be emphasized. *(Stop now!)*	
Commands do not require a time indicator after the verbs to be emphasized *(Take out the trash).*			Commands can be formed by adding a time indicator after the verbs to be emphasized. *(Take out the trash at 9:00.)*	
Commands use consistent verb form (Show it to me).				Commands can be formed by changing the verb ending *(Show[ing] it to me).*
NEGATIVES AND NEGATIVE SENTENCES				
Double negatives are not used *(She doesn't eat anything).*	Double negatives are routinely used to reinforce the thought *(She doesn't eat nothing).*			
The negative marker goes after the verb phrase *(They have not been there before).*	The negative marker goes before the verb phrase *(They not have been there before.).*		The negative marker goes before the verb phrase *(They not have been there before.)*	The negative marker goes before the verb phrase *(They not have been there before).*

AR72 Additional Resources

©2018 Benchmark Education Company, LLC

Contrastive Analysis of English and Nine World Languages

English Grammar	Korean	Cantonese	Mandarin	Farsi	Arabic
QUESTIONS					
Yes/No questions usually begin with a question word. *(Do you eat broccoli? Is this your sweater?)*	Yes/No questions can be formed by adding an element to the end of a declarative statement *(You eat broccoli, yes? This is your sweater, no?)*	Yes/No questions can be formed by adding an element to the end of a declarative statement. *(You eat broccoli, yes? This is your sweater, no?)*	Yes/No questions can be formed by adding an element to the end of a declarative statement. *(You eat broccoli, yes? This is your sweater, no?)*	Yes/No questions can be formed by adding an element to the end of a declarative statement. *(You eat broccoli, yes? This is your sweater, no?)*	Yes/No questions can be formed by adding "or not" to the end of a declarative statement. *(You eat broccoli, or not? This is your sweater, or not?)*
Yes/No questions can be formed by adding a verb followed by its negative at the end of a statement. *(Do you like to go to the beach or not?)*		Yes/No questions can be formed by adding a verb followed by its negative within a statement. *(Do you not like to go to the beach?)*	Yes/No questions can be formed by adding a verb followed by its negative within a statement. *(Do you not like to go to the beach?)*		
Questions words are usually placed at the beginning of the sentence. *(Where is the book? What did my sister tell you?)*	Question words are placed according to the position of the answer. For example, if the answer functions as an object, the question words are placed in the regular object position *(The book is where? My sister told you what?)*	Question words are placed according to the position of the answer. For example, if the answer functions as an object, the question words are placed in the regular object position. *(The book is where? My sister told you what?)*	Question words are placed according to the position of the answer. For example, if the answer functions as an object, the question words are placed in the regular object position. *(The book is where? My sister told you what?)*	Question words are placed according to the position of the answer. For example, if the answer functions as an object, the question words are placed in the regular object position. *(The book is where? My sister told you what?)*	
Yes and no answers are used in a consistent manner. *(Do you play soccer? Yes. Do you play hockey? No.)*				The answers yes and no vary depending upon the verb used in the question. Students may substitute a verb for a yes-no answer *(Do you play soccer? Soccer. Do you play hockey? No hockey.)*	
COMMANDS					
Commands are formed consistently. *(Stop it now!)*			Commands can be formed by adding an adverb after the verbs to be emphasized. *(Stop now!)*		
Commands do not require a time indicator after the verbs to be emphasized *(Take out the trash).*			Commands can be formed by adding a time indicator after the verbs to be emphasized *(Take out the trash at 9:00).*	Commands can be formed by adding a time indicator after the verbs to be emphasized *(Take out the trash at 9:00).*	
Commands use consistent verb form *(Show it to me).*			Commands can be formed by changing the verb ending *(Show[ing] it to me).*	Commands can be formed by changing the verb ending *(Show[ing] it to me).*	
NEGATIVES AND NEGATIVE SENTENCES					
Double negatives are not used *(She doesn't eat anything).*		Double negation is usually used in reverted sentence order with "nothing" and a word of emphasis before the verb *(They nothing have not been there before).*	Double negation is usually used in reverted sentence order with "nothing" and a word of emphasis before the verb *(They nothing have not been there before).*	Double negatives are routinely used *(She doesn't eat nothing).*	Double negatives are sometimes used. *(He doesn't drink coffee never).*
The negative marker goes after the verb phrase *(They have not been there before).*	The negative marker goes before the verb phrase *(They not have been there before)* Korean: used regularly in informal situations.			The negative marker goes before the verb phrase *(They not have been there before).*	

©2018 Benchmark Education Company, LLC

Contrastive Analysis of English and Nine World Languages

Syntax and Grammar: Adverbs and Adjectives
Differences and Potential Errors for English Learners

English Grammar	Spanish	Vietnamese	Hmong	Tagalog
ADVERBS				
Use of adverbs to describe an adjective or a verb (*I ate <u>really</u> fast. I ran <u>quickly</u> to the store*).			Adverbs are not used. Two adjectives or two verbs can be used to describe an adjective or verb (*I ate <u>fast fast</u>. I <u>ran ran</u> to the store*).	
ADJECTIVES				
Adjectives precede nouns they modify (*We live in a <u>coastal</u> city. She has a <u>yellow</u> shirt.*)	Adjectives follow nouns they modify (*We live in a city <u>coastal</u>. She has a shirt <u>yellow</u>*). The adjective position can also reflect meaning.	Adjectives follow nouns they modify (*We live in a city <u>coastal</u>. She has a shirt <u>yellow</u>*).	Adjectives follow nouns they modify (*We live in a city coastal. She has a shirt <u>yellow</u>*).	
Use of **possessive adjectives** used to indicate ownership (*This is <u>her</u> sweater. She wears <u>her</u> sweater*).		Omission of possessive adjectives when ownership is clear (*She wears sweater*).	Use of another word, article or character used to indicate ownership (*This is <u>she</u> sweater*).	
Comparative adjectives change form (*He is <u>taller than</u> me. They are <u>slower than</u> him*).	Comparative adjectives change form (*He is <u>more tall</u> than me. They are <u>more slow</u> than him*).		Comparative adjectives change form (*He is <u>more tall</u> than me. They are <u>more slow</u> than him*).	Comparative adjectives change form (*He is <u>more tall</u> than me. They are <u>more slow</u> than him*).
Nouns and adjectives have different forms (*They want to be <u>independent</u>*).				
Adjectives do not reflect gender or number of nouns they modify (*They have <u>sharp</u> teeth*).	Adjectives reflect gender and number of nouns they modify (*They have <u>sharps</u> teeth*).			Adjectives reflect gender and number of nouns they modify (*They have <u>sharps</u> teeth*).
Use of **possessive adjectives** used for parts of the body (*The boy skinned <u>his</u> knee*).	Use of definite article instead of possessive adjectives used for parts of the body (*The boy skinned <u>the</u> knee*).			
Distinction between personal pronouns and possessive adjectives (*This is <u>my</u> friend*).		Distinction between personal pronouns and possessive adjectives (*This is friend I*).		

AR74　Additional Resources

©2018 Benchmark Education Company, LLC

Contrastive Analysis of English and Nine World Languages

Common Core Language Standard 1:

Demonstrate command of the conventions of standard English grammar and usage when writing or speaking.

L.1.1f Use frequently occurring adjectives.
L.2.1e Use adjectives and adverbs, and choose between them depending on what is to be modified.
L.3.1g Form and use comparative and superlative adjectives and adverbs, and choose between them depending on what is to be modified.
L.4.1a Use interrogative, relative pronouns (who, whose, whom, which, that) and relative adverbs (where, when, why). CA
L.4.1d Order adjectives within sentences according to conventional patterns (e.g., a small red bag rather than a red small bag).

English Grammar	Korean	Cantonese	Mandarin	Farsi	Arabic
ADVERBS					
Use of adverbs to describe an adjective or a verb *(I ate really fast. I ran quickly to the store).*					
ADJECTIVES					
Adjectives precede nouns they modify *(We live in a coastal city. She has a yellow shirt).*				Adjectives follow nouns they modify *(We live in a city coastal. She has a shirt yellow).* The adjective position can also reflect meaning.	Adjectives follow the nouns they modify.
Use of **possessive adjectives** used to indicate ownership *(This is her sweater. She wears her sweater).*	Omission of possessive adjectives when ownership is clear *(She wears sweater).*	Use of another word, article or character used to indicate ownership *(This is she sweater).*	Use of another word, article or character used to indicate ownership *(This is she sweater).*		
Comparative adjectives change form *(He is taller than me. They are slower than him).*	Comparative adjectives change form *(He is more tall than me. They are more slow than him).*				
Nouns and adjectives have different forms *(They want to be independent).*		Some nouns and adjectives use the same forms *(They want to be independence).*	Some nouns and adjectives use the same forms *(They want to be independence.)*		
Adjectives do not reflect gender or number of nouns they modify *(They have sharp teeth).*					Adjectives agree with the gender and number of nouns they modify.
Use of **possessive adjectives** used for parts of the body *(The boy skinned his knee).*					
Distinction between personal pronouns and possessive adjectives *(This is my friend).*					

©2018 Benchmark Education Company, LLC

Additional Resources **AR75**

Contrastive Analysis of English and Nine World Languages

Syntax and Grammar: Pronouns
Differences and Potential Errors for English Learners

English Grammar	Spanish	Vietnamese	Hmong	Tagalog
PRONOUNS				
Distinction between **subject and object pronouns** (*He gave it to me. We spent the time with her*).	No distinction between subject and object pronouns (*He gave it to I. We spent the time with she.*)	No distinction between subject and object pronouns (*He gave it to I. We spent the time with she*).	No distinction between subject and object pronouns (*He gave it to I. We spent the time with she*).	
Distinction between **subject and object** forms of pronouns (*I gave the book to him*).	No distinction between subject and object forms of pronouns (*I gave the book to he*).		No distinction between subject and object forms of pronouns (*I gave the book to he.*)	
Use of **pronoun "it" as a subject** (*It is four o'clock now. What time is it?*)		Optional use of pronoun "it" as a subject (*Four o'clock now. What time?*)	Optional use of pronoun "it" as a subject. (*Four o'clock now. What time?*)	Optional use of pronoun "it" as a subject. (*Four o'clock now. What time?*)
Distinction between **object, subject, simple, compound, and reflexive pronouns** (*He is my cousin. The pencil is mine. I can do it by myself*).		Reflexive pronoun is formed by adding "oneself" to the verb phrase.	No distinction between object, subject, simple, compound, and reflexive pronouns (*He is I cousin. The pencil is I. I can do it I.*)	
Use of **gender specific third person singular pronouns** (*Go talk to the man and ask him for directions*).	No use of gender specific third person singular pronouns (*Go talk to the man and ask it for directions*).	No use of gender specific third person singular pronouns (*Go talk to the man and ask it for directions*). Vietnamese uses familiar form of third person singular.	No use of gender specific third person singular pronouns (*Go talk to the man and ask it for directions*).	No use of gender specific third person singular pronouns (*Go talk to the man and ask it for directions*).
Use of **relative pronouns** (*Go get the book that is on the desk. If you want to drive, there are three ways to get there*).		No use of relative pronouns (*Go get the book is on the desk*).		
Use of **human/nonhuman distinction for relative pronouns** (who/which) (*She is the one who wants to go. The neighbors who just moved in are at the door*).	*Quien* is a relative pronoun used specifically for humans.		No human/nonhuman distinction for relative pronouns (who/which) (*She is the one which wants to go. The neighbors which just moved in are at the door*).	
Use of **possessive pronouns** to indicate ownership (*The shorts are his. These snacks are theirs*).		A separate word or character is used before a pronoun to indicate ownership (*The shorts are (of) him. These snacks are [of] them*). Omission of possessive pronoun when association is clear (He raised his hand).	Use of a possessive character between pronoun and noun to indicate ownership (*He [possessive character] shorts. Snacks [possessive character] them*). Possessive pronoun can come after the noun. Omission of possessive pronoun when association is clear (He raised his hand).	
Personal pronouns are not restated (*Your sister wants to go too*).				
No use of **pronoun object at the end of a relative clause** (*The mouse that ran by was small*).				

AR76 Additional Resources

©2018 Benchmark Education Company, LLC

Contrastive Analysis of English and Nine World Languages

Common Core Language Standard 1:
Demonstrate command of the conventions of standard English grammar and usage when writing or speaking.

L.1.1d Use personal (subject, object), possessive, and indefinite pronouns (e.g., I, me, my; they, them, their; anyone, everything). CA
L.2.1c Use reflexive pronouns (e.g., myself, ourselves)
L.3.1k Use reciprocal pronouns correctly. CA
L.4.1a Use interrogative, relative pronouns (who, whose, whom, which, that) and relative adverbs (where, when, why). CA

English Grammar	Korean	Cantonese	Mandarin	Farsi	Arabic
PRONOUNS					
Distinction between **subject and object pronouns** (*He gave it to me. We spent the time with her*).		No distinction between subject and object pronouns (*He gave it to I. We spent the time with she*).	No distinction between subject and object pronouns (*He gave it to I. We spent the time with she*).	No distinction between subject and object pronouns (*He gave it to I. We spent the time with she*).	
Distinction between **subject and object** forms of pronouns (*I gave the book to him*).	No distinction between subject and object forms of pronouns (*I gave the book to he*).		No distinction between subject and object forms of pronouns (*I gave the book to he*).	No distinction between subject and object forms of pronouns (*I gave the book to he*).	
Use of **pronoun "it" as a subject** (*It is four o'clock now. What time is it?*)	Optional use of pronoun "it" as a subject. (Four o'clock now. What time?)	Optional use of pronoun "it" as a subject. (Four o'clock now. What time?)	Optional use of pronoun "it" as a subject. (Four o'clock now. What time?)		
Distinction between **object, subject, simple, compound, and reflexive pronouns** (*He is my cousin. The pencil is mine. I can do it by myself*).		Uses possession words to distinguish.	Uses possession words to distinguish.		
Use of **gender specific third person singular pronouns** (*Go talk to the man and ask him for directions*).		No use of gender specific third person singular pronouns (*Go talk to the man and ask it for directions*).	No use of gender specific third person singular pronouns (*Go talk to the man and ask it for directions*).	No use of gender specific third person singular pronouns (*Go talk to the man and ask it for directions*).	
Use of **relative pronouns** (*Go get the book that is on the desk. If you want to drive, there are three ways to get there*).	No use of relative pronouns (*Go get the book is on the desk. If you want to drive, three ways to get there*). In Korean, a modifying clause can function as a relative clause.				
Use of **human/nonhuman distinction for relative pronouns** (who/which) (*She is the one who wants to go. The neighbors who just moved in are at the door*).				No human/nonhuman distinction for relative pronouns (who/which) (*She is the one which wants to go. The neighbors which just moved in are at the door*).	No human/nonhuman distinction for relative pronouns (who/which) (*She is the one which wants to go. The neighbors which just moved in are at the door*).
Use of **possessive pronouns** to indicate ownership (*The shorts are his. These snacks are theirs*).	Omission of possessive pronoun when association is clear (*He raised his hand*).	Use of a possessive character between pronoun and noun to indicate ownership (*He (possessive character) shorts. Snacks (possessive character) them.*) Character sometimes omitted.	Use of a possessive character between pronoun and noun to indicate ownership (*He [possessive character] shorts. Snacks [possessive character] them*). Omission of possessive character when association is clear or to limit redundancy (*He raised [possessive character] hand*).	No distinction between personal and possessive pronouns (*The shorts are him. These snacks are they*).	
Personal pronouns are not restated (*Your sister wants to go too*).					Personal pronouns are restated (*Your sister she wants to go too*).
No use of **pronoun object at the end of a relative clause** (*The mouse that ran by was small*).					Pronoun object added at the end of a relative clause (*The mouse that ran by it was small*).

©2018 Benchmark Education Company, LLC

Additional Resources **AR77**

Contrastive Analysis of English and Nine World Languages

Syntax and Grammar:
Prepositions, Conjunctions, Articles
Differences and Potential Errors for English Learners

English Grammar	Spanish	Vietnamese	Hmong	Tagalog
PREPOSITIONS				
Use of prepositions (*The movie is on the DVD*).	Use of prepositions may be different than in English (*The movie is in the DVD*).			
CONJUNCTIONS				
Only one conjunction is needed (*Although, I know her, I don't know what she likes. OR I know her but I don't know what she likes*).				
ARTICLES				
Use of articles.			Classifiers take the place of articles in Hmong.	
Use of **indefinite articles** (*I bought an orange. Do they go to a market for groceries?*)		No use of indefinite articles (*I bought one orange. Do they go to market for groceries?*)	Plural form of classifiers take the place of articles. (*I bought one orange. Do they go to market for groceries?*)	
Use of **indefinite articles** before a profession (*She is a brilliant scientist. He is an electrician*).	Use of indefinite articles before a profession is optional (*She is brilliant scientist. He is electrician*).	No use of indefinite articles before a profession (*She is brilliant scientist. He is electrician*).	In Hmong, professions have unique classifiers, although some are shared. (*She is brilliant scientist. He is electrician.*)	
Consistent use of **definite articles** (*I have the piece of paper. She has a pencil*).	Definite articles can be omitted or used (*I have [a] piece of paper. She has [a] pencil*).		Definite articles can be omitted. (*I have piece of paper. She has pencil.*)	Definite articles can be omitted (*I have piece of paper. She has pencil*).
No use of **definite article** for generalization (*Eating vegetables is healthful for people*).	Use of definite article for generalization (*Eating the vegetables is healthful for the people*).		Use of definite article for generalization (*Eating the vegetables is healthful for the people*).	Use of definite article for generalization (*Eating the vegetables is healthful for the people*).
No use of **definite articles** with a profession (*Doctor Sanchez is at the hospital*).	Optional use of definite articles with a profession (*The Doctor Sanchez is at the hospital*).		Optional use of definite articles with a profession (*The Doctor Sanchez is at the hospital*).	Optional use of definite articles with a profession (*The Doctor Sanchez is at the hospital*).
No use of **definite articles** with months, sometimes not used with places (*We will go in May. She is in bed*).	Use of definite article with months, sometimes not used with places. (*We will go in the May. She is in the bed.*)		Use of definite article with months, sometimes not used with places. (*We will go in the May. She is in the bed.*)	

AR78 Additional Resources

©2018 Benchmark Education Company, LLC

Contrastive Analysis of English and Nine World Languages

Common Core Language Standard 1:
Demonstrate command of the conventions of standard English grammar and usage when writing or speaking.

L.K.1e Use the most frequently occurring prepositions (e.g., to, from, in, out, on, off, for, of, by, with).
L.1.1g Use frequently occurring conjunctions (e.g., and, but, or, so, because).
L.1.1h Use determiners (e.g., articles, demonstratives).
L.1.1i Use frequently occurring prepositions (e.g., during, beyond, toward).
L.3.1h Use coordinating and subordinating conjunctions.
L.4.1e Form and use prepositional phrases.
L.5.1e Use correlative conjunctions (e.g., either/ or, neither/nor).

English Grammar	Korean	Cantonese	Mandarin	Farsi	Arabic
PREPOSITIONS					
Use of prepositions (*The movie is on the DVD*).					
CONJUNCTIONS					
Only one conjunction is needed (*Although, I know her, I don't know what she likes. OR I know her but I don't know what she likes*).		Conjunctions occur in pairs (*Although, I know her but I don't know what she likes*).	Conjunctions occur in pairs (*Although, I know her but I don't know what she likes*).		Coordination favored over subordination (frequent use of <u>and</u> and <u>so</u>).
ARTICLES					
Use of articles.		Use of articles to be very clear and definite.	Use of articles to be very clear and definite.	No use of articles.	
Use of **indefinite articles** (*I bought an orange. Do they go to a market for groceries?*)	No use of indefinite articles (*I bought <u>one</u> orange. Do they go to <u>a</u> market for groceries?*) Depends on the context.	No use of indefinite articles (*I bought <u>one</u> orange at the store. Do they go to one market for groceries?*)	No use of indefinite articles (*I bought <u>one</u> orange at the store. Do they go to one market for groceries?*)		No use of indefinite articles (*I bought one orange. Do they go to market for groceries?*)
Use of **indefinite articles** before a profession (*She is a brilliant scientist. He is an electrician*).	No use of indefinite articles before a profession (*She is brilliant scientist. He is electrician*).	No use of indefinite articles before a profession (*She is brilliant scientist. He is electrician*).	No use of indefinite articles before a profession (*She is brilliant scientist. He is electrician*).	No use of indefinite articles before a profession (*She is brilliant scientist. He is electrician*).	No use of indefinite articles before a profession (*She is brilliant scientist. He is electrician*).
Consistent use of **definite articles** (*I have <u>the</u> piece of paper. She has <u>a</u> pencil*).		Definite articles can be omitted (*I have piece of paper. She has pencil*).	Definite articles can be omitted (*I have piece of paper. She has pencil*).		
No use of **definite article** for generalization (*Eating vegetables is healthful for people*).					
No use of **definite articles** with a profession (*Doctor Sanchez is at the hospital*).				Optional use of definite articles with a profession (*<u>The</u> Doctor Sanchez is at the hospital*).	The definite article is used with names of professions before a proper noun (*The Doctor Sanchez is at the hospital*).
No use of **definite articles** with months, sometimes not used with places (*We will go in May. She is in bed*).					Use of definite article with days, months, places, idioms (*We will go in <u>the</u> May. She is in <u>the</u> bed*).

©2018 Benchmark Education Company, LLC

Additional Resources   **AR79**

Vocabulary Charts with Spanish Cognates

Unit 3

Week	Vocabulary Words*	
1	big **gigantic (gigantesco)** huge large **enormous (enorme)** **delicious (delicioso)** tasty cold freezing chilly hot dry sizzling warm fiery sun-baked burnt dusty large	tired **exhausted (exhausto)** drowsy sleepy use usar few cute **cube (cubo)** **music (música)** **rescue (rescate)** **menu (menú)** fuel January barren **desert (desierto)** **fragile (frágil)** harsh huddle
2	**habitat (hábitat)** grasslands prairie **savanna (sabana)** blubber **tundra (tundra)** **coral (coral)** **car (carro)** star **march (marcha)** smart hard farm large shark garden yard shallow thaws	
3	loud earsplitting cool freezing quiet **silent (silente, silencioso)** hushed peaceful hot hungry starving happy delighted afraid **terrified (aterrado)** silly goofy	

Unit 4

Week	Vocabulary Words*	
1	**admired (admirado)** before boasted born fork happily horn more oars **probably (probablemente)** quickly roar sports store suddenly **unique (único)** wore	
2	beg begged begged breathe in cheer clear claro deer **delicious (delicioso)** dropped ears fear feast hear here mix	near rubbed sample share sip smell sniff spare steer stir swirl taste tasty whispered year
3	bear care chair deal **direction (dirección)** encouragement hair **insulted (insultó)** lot pear plus **rose (rosa)** rubble share side **sign (signo)** square stairs tidy wear where	

*Words in parentheses are Spanish cognates

Managing an Independent Reading Program

Independent reading is a critical component of the *Benchmark Advance* literacy block. It is the time during which students experience the joy of reading self-selected books based on their interests and reading abilities.

As students read widely, both literary and content-rich informational texts, they increase their background knowledge and understanding of the world; they increase their vocabulary and familiarity with varied grammatical and text organizational structures; they build habits for reading and stamina; they practice their reading skills; and perhaps, most importantly, they discover interests they can carry forward into a lifetime of reading and enjoying books and texts of all types.

Within *Benchmark Advance,* students may participate in daily independent reading during the Independent and Collaborative Activity block, while the teacher meets with small groups of students to conduct differentiated small-group reading instruction, model fluency skills through Reader's Theater, or reteach skills and strategies.

Explicit support for managing independent reading is provided in the online component *Managing Your Independent Reading Program*. This resource is available to read and/or download at benchmarkuniverse.com. It provides:

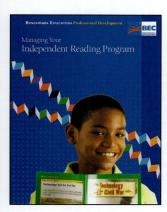

- guidance for setting up and managing a classroom reading program;
- strategies to help students self-select books and texts;
- ideas to support book-sharing, partner-reading, and discussion circles;
- activities to promote reflection and writing in response to reading;
- prompts, questions, and strategies to support engaging one-on-one conferencing between teacher and student;
- home-school letters.

Students may draw from many sources for independent reading including classroom-library and school-library books. In addition, a list of recommended, award-winning trade books is provided for every unit in *Benchmark Advance* (at the end of this section), with titles that expand on the unit concepts and essential questions.

Recommended Trade Books

Unit 3: Plants and Animals in Their Habitats

Title	Author	Genre	Summary Notes	Awards
On the Move: Mass Migrations	Scotti Cohn	Informational Nonfiction	This book helps readers explore animal migration. Readers will learn about many different animal habitats and animals' eating, hibernating, and breeding behaviors.	Horn Book Guide Titles Rated 1–4 Outstanding Science Trade Books for Students K–12
Egg: Nature's Perfect Package	Robin Page & Steve Jenkins	Informational Nonfiction	This book describes different types of animal eggs. Readers will learn about the types of animals who begin life as eggs and whose babies grow in eggs. It describes how many eggs each animal lays and how they protect them.	Outstanding Science Trade Books for Students K–12 Starred Reviews
The Fruits We Eat	Gail Gibbons	Informational Nonfiction	This text provides details about how fruits grow, how fruit is harvested, and which parts of fruit are planted to produce more. It also discusses the difference between large industrial farms and small fruit growers, fruit processing and transportation, and fresh produce available in stores and on farm stands.	2016 Outstanding Science Trade Books for Students K–12, Starred Reviews
Waiting for Ice	Sandra Markle	Narrative Nonfiction	This is a true story about an orphaned 10-month-old polar bear cub who was left to survive on her own on Wrangel Island in the Arctic Ocean.	2013 Outstanding Science Trade Book for Students K–12
Neighborhood Sharks: Hunting with the Great Whites of California's Farallon Islands	Katherine Roy	Narrative Nonfiction	This story is about the great white sharks who come to feed at the Farallon Islands near San Francisco and the scientists who study them.	Rated 1–4 Library Media Connection Starred Reviews Outstanding Science Trade Books for Students K–12 Teachers' Choices Robert F. Sibert Informational Book Medal (2015) SLJ Best Books 2014, Nonfiction Kirkus Reviews Best Books of 2014, Picture Books New York Public Library, 100 Titles for Reading and Sharing 2014, Nonfiction 2015 NCTE Orbis Pictus Recommended Book ALA Notable Books for Children 2015, Middle Readers NSTA Outstanding Science Trade Books for Students K–12: 2015 CBC Children's Choice Book Awards 2015 Finalist, Debut Author Horn Book Fanfare List: Best Books of 2014, Nonfiction 2015 John Burroughs Riverby Award
Butterfly Eyes and Other Secrets of the Meadows	Joyce Sidman	Informational Poetry	This book combines poetry and informational text to describe living things in a meadow. The poems are riddles that describe a living thing and end with a question asking readers to figure out who or what they are.	Starred Reviews Children's Notable Books Kirkus Books of Special Note Outstanding Science Trade Books for Students K–12
The Great Kapok Tree: A Tale of the Amazon Rain Forest	Lynne Cherry	Animal Fantasy	This book takes a look at what the Kapok tree means to the creatures that live in it and what rain forests mean to the world's ecology.	Children's Core Collection, 20th ed. and Supplements

Recommended Trade Books

Unit 4: Many Characters, Many Points of View

Title	Author	Genre	Summary Notes	Awards
Dear Primo: Letter to My Cousin	Duncan Tonatiuh	Realistic Fiction	This book explores the differences between two cultures. Two boy cousins write letters to each other. One boy lives in Mexico and the other boy lives in New York City. The boys describe in their letters what their lives are like and what they do.	Children's Notable Books Pura Belpre Awards
Mercy Watson Goes for a Ride	Kate DiCamillo	Fiction	A pig, Mercy, and her owners are driving around one Saturday. The family eats a big breakfast and then Mercy and Mr. Watson take a ride in his convertible. On this particular Saturday things do not go as planned. Readers will enjoy the humorous tone of this story about a pig who tries to drive a convertible.	Theodor Seuss Geisel Nominee
Bink and Gollie	Kate DiCamillo	Fiction	Bink and Gollie are two young girls who are best friends. In this book readers will experience three of Bink and Gollie's adventures together.	National Book Award Nominee for Young People's Literature (2013) Theodor Seuss Geisel Award (2011) Publishers Weekly's Best Children's Books of the Year for Fiction (2010) Goodreads Choice Award Nominee for Picture Book (2010)
Any Questions?	Marie-Louise Gay	Realistic Fiction	In this book the author answers questions about what she writes about and how she comes up with her ideas. She goes through the process of brainstorming and then goes on to write a short story.	Winner of the Amelia Frances Howard-Gibbon Illustrator's Award Finalist for the Governor General's Literary Award for Children's Illustration Finalist for the TD Canadian Children's Literature Award Finalist for the Quebec Writers' Federation Prize for Children's and Young Adult Literature Finalist for the Vancouver Children's Roundtable Information Book Award A School Library Journal Best Book of the Year A Kirkus Reviews Best Book of the Year A Cooperative Children's Book Center Choice A White Ravens Selection A Globe 100 Best Book Notable Children's Books in the Language Arts
Piper Green and the Fairy Tree	Ellen Potter	Fiction	Piper is a second grade girl who lives on a small island off the coast of Maine. She takes a boat to school every day with her younger brother. This book gives a realistic portrayal of a second grader's way of dealing with life changes.	2015 Junior Library Guild, Starred reviews
I'm My Own Dog	David Ezra Stein	Fiction	A dog's narrative about how he is his own dog who eventually finds a person whom he takes for walks, tells him to sit on a park bench, cleans up after him, and how he's grown quite attached to his "little fella." A great example of perspective with a humorous twist and fun, colorful, childlike drawings.	Vermont's Picture Book Awards: Red Clover Nominee (2016) The Magnolia Award Nominee for K-2 (2016) Starred Reviews
I Want My Hat Back	Jon Klassen	Animal Fantasy	When a bear cannot find his beloved hat, he becomes determined to figure out what happened to it. He asks every animal he comes across if they have seen his hat, but it is the one question asked of him that triggers his memory and leads to the hat's recovery.	Deutscher Jugendliteraturpreis for Bilderbuch (2013) Theodor Seuss Geisel Honor (2012) Irma Black Award Nominee (2012) Selezionato Mostra Internazionale d'illustrazione per l'infanzia di Sarmede (2011) E. B. White Read Aloud Winner 2012

©2018 Benchmark Education Company, LLC